GUNFIGHTER®

FUNDAMENTAL PISTOL

WARM UPS, DRILLS, EXERCISES AND QUALS

NAME: _____   UNIT: _____

Weapon Conditions

- Condition 4: No mag inserted. Slide forward on empty chamber. Hammer forward (if applicable). Weapon on safe (if applicable).

- Condition 3: Loaded mag inserted. Slide forward on empty chamber. Hammer forward (if applicable). Weapon on safe (if applicable).

- Condition 2: Loaded mag inserted. Slide forward with round in chamber. Hammer forward (if applicable). Weapon on safe (if applicable).

- Condition 1: Loaded mag inserted. Slide forward with round in chamber. Hammer cocked (if applicable). Weapon on safe (if applicable).

Always know the condition of your weapon!

Safety

- Treat every weapon as if it were loaded.

- Never point your weapon at anything you do not intend to shoot/destroy.

- Know your target and it's background.

- Keep your finger off the trigger until you intend to fire.

- Keep your weapon on safe until you are ready to fire.

- Always wear eye and ear protection, and proper protective clothing.

- Never shoot faster than you can effectively keep rounds on target.

- Be extremely cautious with back splatter and ricochets when shooting steel.

Warning

Perform these drills at your own risk. Only perform these drill in a safe manner which do not violate your range rules. Consult range staff for rules and regulations regarding drawing from a holster, rapid fire and multiple target engagements.

GUNFIGHTER is not responsible for any injury or death that may occur due to the use of this book. We recommend never shooting alone and under supervision of trained safety officers.

Table of Contents:

How to use this book:

This book offers a carefully crafted catalog of training drills and is designed to log and track training progression as well as shot pattern placement analysis. **All targets may be downloaded for free** of our www.GunfighterSeries.com website and printed at home for free with the exception of the JD-QUAL1 target which may be purchased at numerous online retailers. The JD-Qual1 target may also be substituted with a carboard IPSC with a rectangular body A zone.

For best results, conduct and record every drill at least once starting at the beginning. The more data you collect the better your results will be.

Most drills offer defensive time and scoring goals to achieve. Competitive shooters may set different goals. Everyone's goal should be to improve their recorded personal best.

For proper weapons handling and marksmanship coaching, seek out well respected firearms instructors and courses.

Train safe. Train hard. Train to win.

Afterwards:

Upon mastering all the drills in this book, continue to increase your skills by utilizing the entire Gunfighter training log book series.

ISBN: 9781072800699   Revised 2019

Round Count Log

Weapon Make & Model: _____   SN#: _____

Date	Ammo	Lot #	Fired	Total

Date	Ammo	Lot #	Fired	Total

Notes:

This Page	
Previous Page	
TOTAL	

Round Count Log

Weapon Make & Model: _____   SN#: _____

Date	Ammo	Lot #	Fired	Total		Date	Ammo	Lot #	Fired	Total

Notes:

	This Page	
	Previous Page	
	TOTAL	

Round Count Log

Weapon Make & Model: SN#:

Date	Ammo	Lot #	Fired	Total

Date	Ammo	Lot #	Fired	Total

Notes:

This Page	
Previous Page	
TOTAL	

Round Count Log

Weapon Make & Model: _____   SN#: _____

Date	Ammo	Lot #	Fired	Total		Date	Ammo	Lot #	Fired	Total

Notes:

This Page	
Previous Page	
TOTAL	

Maintenance Log

Weapon Make & Model: _____   SN#: _____

Date	Full Cleaning	Damage Inspection
	Y / N	Y / N
	Y / N	Y / N
	Y / N	Y / N
	Y / N	Y / N
	Y / N	Y / N
	Y / N	Y / N
	Y / N	Y / N
	Y / N	Y / N
	Y / N	Y / N
	Y / N	Y / N
	Y / N	Y / N
	Y / N	Y / N
	Y / N	Y / N
	Y / N	Y / N

Parts Replaced:

Date	Full Cleaning	Damage Inspection
	Y / N	Y / N
	Y / N	Y / N
	Y / N	Y / N
	Y / N	Y / N
	Y / N	Y / N
	Y / N	Y / N
	Y / N	Y / N
	Y / N	Y / N
	Y / N	Y / N
	Y / N	Y / N
	Y / N	Y / N
	Y / N	Y / N
	Y / N	Y / N
	Y / N	Y / N

Notes:

DRAW 1, 2, 3

Purpose: Increase speed of draw stroke.

Distance: 5 Yards.

Target: JD-QUAL1

Par Time: N / A

Total Rounds Fired: 0 Rounds.

Repetitions: 10 Reps.

Starting Position & Condition: See description . Condition 4.

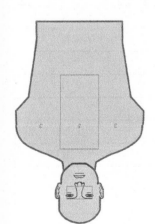

"Draw 1" Description: With hands up in front of you, at your personal go, take your dominant hand/arm, bring your elbow straight back and clear your concealment garment (if you have one) with your dominant hand and establish a good grip on the pistol. As your bring your dominant hand back to clear a garment and/or establish a good pistol grip, move your support hand to your chest with that hand's palm facing your chest. As you perform your dry repetitions, try to be smooth and deliberate. Re-peat for 10 reps.

"Draw 2" Description: With your support hand in front of your chest, palm facing toward your chest and your dominant hand on the pistol with a good pistol grip, at your personal go, draw the pistol straight up just under your arm pit. Rotate pistol toward the target and bring your support hand onto the dominant hand establishing a good two handed pistol grip. As you perform your dry repetitions, try to be smooth and deliberate. Repeat for 10 reps.

"Draw 3" Description: Starting from the ending position of the Draw 2 drill, at your personal go, press the pistol out in front of you bring it up in line with your eye to a point where you are aiming at the spot on your target. When your pistol reaches the end of the presentation; press the trigger. The point of this, is to get you use to firing quickly while getting a flash sight picture of your front sight.   Repeat for 10 reps.

DRAW DRY

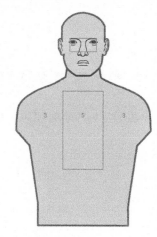

Purpose: Increase speed of draw stroke.

Distance: 5 Yards.

Target: JD-QUAL1

Par Time: 2 seconds non-concealed, 2.5 seconds concealed.

Extra equipment required: Shot timer.

Total Rounds Fired: 0 Rounds.

Point Penalty: N / A

Repetitions: 10 Reps.

Starting Position & Condition: Standing Surrender / Interview. Condition 4.

"Draw Dry" Description: At the timer beep, perform a complete drawing of your pistol as through Draw 1-3 exercises and dry fire as you did in Draw 3.

Goals: The goal of this par time is to be smooth and deliberate.

DRAW DRY RIGHT & LEFT

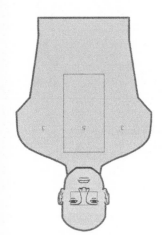

Purpose: To get out of the line of attack and attack when drawing a pistol for defense.

Distance: 10 Yards.

Target: JD-QUAL1

Extra Equipment Needed: Shot timer.

Par Time: 2.8 Seconds.

Total Rounds Fired: 0 Rounds.

Point Penalty: Go / No Go.

Repetitions: 10 Reps.

Starting Position & Condition: Standing Surrender / Interview. Condition 4.

"Draw Dry Right" Description: At the timer beep, perform a complete draw of your pistol as through Draw 1-3 exercises while moving 1 to 2 steps to the right. This movement is to get you out of the line of fire or attack while moving laterally. Repeat for 10 reps.

"Draw Dry Left" Description: At the timer beep, perform a complete drawing of your pistol as through Draw 1-3 exercises while moving 1 to 2 steps to the left. This movement is to get you out of the line of fire or attack while moving laterally. Repeat for 10 reps.

DRAW 1, 2, 3 SIDESTEP SERIES

Date:	Location:	Weapon:	Sights:
Draw 1 x 10 Reps: Y / N	**Draw 2** x 10 Reps: Y / N	**Draw 3** x 10 Reps: Y / N	**Draw Dry** x 10 Reps: Y / N
Sidestep Right x 10: Y / N	**Sidestep Left** x 10: Y / N	Notes:	

Date:	Location:	Weapon:	Sights:
Draw 1 x 10 Reps: Y / N	**Draw 2** x 10 Reps: Y / N	**Draw 3** x 10 Reps: Y / N	**Draw Dry** x 10 Reps: Y / N
Sidestep Right x 10: Y / N	**Sidestep Left** x 10: Y / N	Notes:	

Date:	Location:	Weapon:	Sights:
Draw 1 x 10 Reps: Y / N	**Draw 2** x 10 Reps: Y / N	**Draw 3** x 10 Reps: Y / N	**Draw Dry** x 10 Reps: Y / N
Sidestep Right x 10: Y / N	**Sidestep Left** x 10: Y / N	Notes:	

Date:	Location:	Weapon:	Sights:
Draw 1 x 10 Reps: Y / N	**Draw 2** x 10 Reps: Y / N	**Draw 3** x 10 Reps: Y / N	**Draw Dry** x 10 Reps: Y / N
Sidestep Right x 10: Y / N	**Sidestep Left** x 10: Y / N	Notes:	

DRAW 1, 2, 3 SIDESTEP SERIES

Date:	Location:	Weapon:	Sights:
Draw 1 x 10 Reps: Y / N	**Draw 2** x 10 Reps: Y / N	**Draw 3** x 10 Reps: Y / N	**Draw Dry** x 10 Reps: Y / N
Sidestep Right x 10: Y / N	**Sidestep Left** x 10: Y / N	Notes:	

Date:	Location:	Weapon:	Sights:
Draw 1 x 10 Reps: Y / N	**Draw 2** x 10 Reps: Y / N	**Draw 3** x 10 Reps: Y / N	**Draw Dry** x 10 Reps: Y / N
Sidestep Right x 10: Y / N	**Sidestep Left** x 10: Y / N	Notes:	

Date:	Location:	Weapon:	Sights:
Draw 1 x 10 Reps: Y / N	**Draw 2** x 10 Reps: Y / N	**Draw 3** x 10 Reps: Y / N	**Draw Dry** x 10 Reps: Y / N
Sidestep Right x 10: Y / N	**Sidestep Left** x 10: Y / N	Notes:	

Date:	Location:	Weapon:	Sights:
Draw 1 x 10 Reps: Y / N	**Draw 2** x 10 Reps: Y / N	**Draw 3** x 10 Reps: Y / N	**Draw Dry** x 10 Reps: Y / N
Sidestep Right x 10: Y / N	**Sidestep Left** x 10: Y / N	Notes:	

DRAW 1, 2, 3 SIDESTEP SERIES

Date:	Location:	Weapon:	Sights:
Draw 1 x 10 Reps: Y / N	**Draw 2** x 10 Reps: Y / N	**Draw 3** x 10 Reps: Y / N	**Draw Dry** x 10 Reps: Y / N
Sidestep Right x 10: Y / N	**Sidestep Left** x 10: Y / N	Notes:	

Date:	Location:	Weapon:	Sights:
Draw 1 x 10 Reps: Y / N	**Draw 2** x 10 Reps: Y / N	**Draw 3** x 10 Reps: Y / N	**Draw Dry** x 10 Reps: Y / N
Sidestep Right x 10: Y / N	**Sidestep Left** x 10: Y / N	Notes:	

Date:	Location:	Weapon:	Sights:
Draw 1 x 10 Reps: Y / N	**Draw 2** x 10 Reps: Y / N	**Draw 3** x 10 Reps: Y / N	**Draw Dry** x 10 Reps: Y / N
Sidestep Right x 10: Y / N	**Sidestep Left** x 10: Y / N	Notes:	

Date:	Location:	Weapon:	Sights:
Draw 1 x 10 Reps: Y / N	**Draw 2** x 10 Reps: Y / N	**Draw 3** x 10 Reps: Y / N	**Draw Dry** x 10 Reps: Y / N
Sidestep Right x 10: Y / N	**Sidestep Left** x 10: Y / N	Notes:	

DRAW 1, 2, 3 SIDESTEP SERIES

Date:	Location:	Weapon:	Sights:
Draw 1 x 10 Reps: Y / N	**Draw 2** x 10 Reps: Y / N	**Draw 3** x 10 Reps: Y / N	**Draw Dry** x 10 Reps: Y / N
Sidestep Right x 10: Y / N	**Sidestep Left** x 10: Y / N	Notes:	

Date:	Location:	Weapon:	Sights:
Draw 1 x 10 Reps: Y / N	**Draw 2** x 10 Reps: Y / N	**Draw 3** x 10 Reps: Y / N	**Draw Dry** x 10 Reps: Y / N
Sidestep Right x 10: Y / N	**Sidestep Left** x 10: Y / N	Notes:	

Date:	Location:	Weapon:	Sights:
Draw 1 x 10 Reps: Y / N	**Draw 2** x 10 Reps: Y / N	**Draw 3** x 10 Reps: Y / N	**Draw Dry** x 10 Reps: Y / N
Sidestep Right x 10: Y / N	**Sidestep Left** x 10: Y / N	Notes:	

Date:	Location:	Weapon:	Sights:
Draw 1 x 10 Reps: Y / N	**Draw 2** x 10 Reps: Y / N	**Draw 3** x 10 Reps: Y / N	**Draw Dry** x 10 Reps: Y / N
Sidestep Right x 10: Y / N	**Sidestep Left** x 10: Y / N	Notes:	

DRAW 1, 2, 3 SIDESTEP SERIES

Date:	Location:	Weapon:	Sights:
Draw 1 x 10 Reps: Y / N	**Draw 2** x 10 Reps: Y / N	**Draw 3** x 10 Reps: Y / N	**Draw Dry** x 10 Reps: Y / N
Sidestep Right x 10: Y / N	**Sidestep Left** x 10: Y / N	Notes:	

Date:	Location:	Weapon:	Sights:
Draw 1 x 10 Reps: Y / N	**Draw 2** x 10 Reps: Y / N	**Draw 3** x 10 Reps: Y / N	**Draw Dry** x 10 Reps: Y / N
Sidestep Right x 10: Y / N	**Sidestep Left** x 10: Y / N	Notes:	

Date:	Location:	Weapon:	Sights:
Draw 1 x 10 Reps: Y / N	**Draw 2** x 10 Reps: Y / N	**Draw 3** x 10 Reps: Y / N	**Draw Dry** x 10 Reps: Y / N
Sidestep Right x 10: Y / N	**Sidestep Left** x 10: Y / N	Notes:	

Date:	Location:	Weapon:	Sights:
Draw 1 x 10 Reps: Y / N	**Draw 2** x 10 Reps: Y / N	**Draw 3** x 10 Reps: Y / N	**Draw Dry** x 10 Reps: Y / N
Sidestep Right x 10: Y / N	**Sidestep Left** x 10: Y / N	Notes:	

LOAD & UNLOAD THAT PISTOL

Purpose: Increase efficiency and develop nervous system memory of loading and unloading a pistol.

Extra Equipment Needed: 5 dummy rounds.

Total Rounds Fired: 5 DUMMY Rounds.

Repetitions: 10 Reps.

Starting Position & Condition: Standing - pistol pointed forward. Condition 4.

Description: Face in a safe direction by following the firearm safety rules. Bring the pistol up in front of your face with your hand just below your eyes so you can maintain situational awareness. Tuck your dominant side elbow into your side. Take a magazine with 5 dummy rounds in it out of your magazine pouch and insert it into the magazine well. After you have inserted the magazine half way; transition from the grip to the palm of your hand pushing on the bottom of the magazine. Push forcefully to the point where you hear the click of the magazine being locked in place. While pointing the pistol in a safe direction, rack the slide to chamber a round. Perform a round press check or check the chambered round indicator to make sure a round is in the chamber. Unload the magazine by locking the slide back, remove the round that was in the chamber and remove the magazine. Perform a 3 point unload safety check.

Goals: To be smooth, deliberate and to remove the round in the chamber first before removing the magazine, allowing you to practice for Type 2 malfunction clearing.

LOAD & UNLOAD THAT PISTOL

Date:	Location:	Weapon:	10 Reps?	Notes:
			Y / N	
			Y / N	
			Y / N	
			Y / N	
			Y / N	
			Y / N	
			Y / N	
			Y / N	
			Y / N	
			Y / N	
			Y / N	
			Y / N	
			Y / N	
			Y / N	
			Y / N	
			Y / N	
			Y / N	
			Y / N	

STACK THAT PISTOL UP

Purpose: Increase efficiency and develop nervous system memory of a **tactical reload.**

Extra Equipment Needed: 2 Magazines.

Total Rounds Fired: 0 Rounds.

Repetitions: 10 Reps.

Starting Position & Condition: Standing - pistol pointed forward. Condition 3 with an empty magazine in the pistol.

Description: Face in a safe direction by following the firearm safety rules. Bring the pistol up in front of your face with your hand just below your eyes, so you can maintain situational awareness. Tuck your dominant side elbow into your side. Take a magazine out of your magazine pouch and hold it between your middle and index finger. Re-move the magazine that is in the pistol with your index finger and thumb. Insert the new magazine into the magazine well. After you have inserted the magazine half way, transition from this grip to the palm of your hand pushing on the bottom of the magazine. Push forcefully to the point where you hear a click of the magazine being locked in place. Insert the magazine that was in the pistol first into the magazine pouch. Perform a scan of the area. If you have more than one magazine pouch, use the magazine from the farthest from the front.

Goals: To be smooth and deliberate.

STACK THAT PISTOL UP

Date:	Location:	Weapon:	10 Reps?	Notes:
			Y / N	
			Y / N	
			Y / N	
			Y / N	
			Y / N	
			Y / N	
			Y / N	
			Y / N	
			Y / N	
			Y / N	
			Y / N	
			Y / N	
			Y / N	
			Y / N	
			Y / N	
			Y / N	
			Y / N	
			Y / N	

GET THAT PISTOL LOADED QUICKLY

Purpose: Increase reloading speed, nervous system memory of an emergency reload and recoil management.

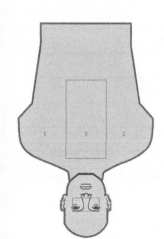

Distance: 10 Yards.

Target: JD-QUAL1

Par Time: 4.5 Seconds.

Extra Equipment Needed: Shot timer, 2 magazines and 1 magazine pouch.

Rounds Fired Per Rep: 3 to 6 Rounds. **Total Rounds Fired:** 15 to 30 Rounds.

Point Penalty: Go / No Go.

Repetitions: 5 Reps.

Starting Position & Condition: Standing - pistol pointed at target. Condition 1 with an empty magazine inserted in the pistol.

Description: At the timer beep, fire 1 round, reload the pistol, aim and fire the 2 to 5 rounds into the A Zone (5 point) body or A Zone (5 point) head box. Record the total time and the reload split time. Repeat 4 more times firing the same number of rounds after reloading as the previous repetitions. Remove the high and low times and average the 3 remaining times for an average. If all rounds impact in the A Zone (5 point) body or head box, mark as a Go. If any rounds are shot out of the A Zone (5 point) body or head box, mark as a No Go.

Goals: Novice: 4.5 Seconds.   Expert: 3.5 Seconds.   Gunfighter: 2.5 Seconds.

Variations: Try different round counts on different sessions and over time, see if your average times for the same round counts are coming down.

GET THAT PISTOL LOADED QUICKLY

Date:	Location:	Weapon:	Sights:	A Box: Head / Body
Rep 1 Time:	Rep 2 Time:	Rep 3 Time:	Rep 4 Time:	Rep 5 Time:
Reload Time:	Reload Time:	Reload Time:	Reload Time:	Reload Time:
A Box: Go / No Go	A Box: Go / No Go	A Box: Go / No Go	A Box: Go / No Go	A Box: Go / No Go
# of Shots:	# of Shots:	# of Shots:	# of Shots:	# of Shots:
Ave Reload Time:		**Ave Total Rep Time:**		Notes:
Date:	Location:	Weapon:	Sights:	A Box: Head / Body
Rep 1 Time:	Rep 2 Time:	Rep 3 Time:	Rep 4 Time:	Rep 5 Time:
Reload Time:	Reload Time:	Reload Time:	Reload Time:	Reload Time:
A Box: Go / No Go	A Box: Go / No Go	A Box: Go / No Go	A Box: Go / No Go	A Box: Go / No Go
# of Shots:	# of Shots:	# of Shots:	# of Shots:	# of Shots:
Ave Reload Time:		**Ave Total Rep Time:**		Notes:
Date:	Location:	Weapon:	Sights:	A Box: Head / Body
Rep 1 Time:	Rep 2 Time:	Rep 3 Time:	Rep 4 Time:	Rep 5 Time:
Reload Time:	Reload Time:	Reload Time:	Reload Time:	Reload Time:
A Box: Go / No Go	A Box: Go / No Go	A Box: Go / No Go	A Box: Go / No Go	A Box: Go / No Go
# of Shots::	# of Shots:	# of Shots:	# of Shots:	# of Shots:
Ave Reload Time:		**Ave Total Rep Time:**		Notes:

GET THAT PISTOL LOADED QUICKLY

Date:	Location:	Weapon:	Sights:	A Box: Head / Body
Rep 1 Time:	Rep 2 Time:	Rep 3 Time:	Rep 4 Time:	Rep 5 Time:
Reload Time:	Reload Time:	Reload Time:	Reload Time:	Reload Time:
A Box: Go / No Go	A Box: Go / No Go	A Box: Go / No Go	A Box: Go / No Go	A Box: Go / No Go
# of Shots:	# of Shots:	# of Shots:	# of Shots:	# of Shots:
Ave Reload Time:		**Ave Total Rep Time:**		Notes:
Date:	Location:	Weapon:	Sights:	A Box: Head / Body
Rep 1 Time:	Rep 2 Time:	Rep 3 Time:	Rep 4 Time:	Rep 5 Time:
Reload Time:	Reload Time:	Reload Time:	Reload Time:	Reload Time:
A Box: Go / No Go	A Box: Go / No Go	A Box: Go / No Go	A Box: Go / No Go	A Box: Go / No Go
# of Shots:	# of Shots:	# of Shots:	# of Shots:	# of Shots:
Ave Reload Time:		**Ave Total Rep Time:**		Notes:
Date:	Location:	Weapon:	Sights:	A Box: Head / Body
Rep 1 Time:	Rep 2 Time:	Rep 3 Time:	Rep 4 Time:	Rep 5 Time:
Reload Time:	Reload Time:	Reload Time:	Reload Time:	Reload Time:
A Box: Go / No Go	A Box: Go / No Go	A Box: Go / No Go	A Box: Go / No Go	A Box: Go / No Go
# of Shots::	# of Shots:	# of Shots:	# of Shots:	# of Shots:
Ave Reload Time:		**Ave Total Rep Time:**		Notes:

GET THAT PISTOL LOADED QUICKLY

Date:	Location:	Weapon:	Sights:	A Box: Head / Body
Rep 1 Time:	Rep 2 Time:	Rep 3 Time:	Rep 4 Time:	Rep 5 Time:
Reload Time:	Reload Time:	Reload Time:	Reload Time:	Reload Time:
A Box: Go / No Go	A Box: Go / No Go	A Box: Go / No Go	A Box: Go / No Go	A Box: Go / No Go
# of Shots:	# of Shots:	# of Shots:	# of Shots:	# of Shots:
Ave Reload Time:		**Ave Total Rep Time:**		Notes:
Date:	Location:	Weapon:	Sights:	A Box: Head / Body
Rep 1 Time:	Rep 2 Time:	Rep 3 Time:	Rep 4 Time:	Rep 5 Time:
Reload Time:	Reload Time:	Reload Time:	Reload Time:	Reload Time:
A Box: Go / No Go	A Box: Go / No Go	A Box: Go / No Go	A Box: Go / No Go	A Box: Go / No Go
# of Shots:	# of Shots:	# of Shots:	# of Shots:	# of Shots:
Ave Reload Time:		**Ave Total Rep Time:**		Notes:
Date:	Location:	Weapon:	Sights:	A Box: Head / Body
Rep 1 Time:	Rep 2 Time:	Rep 3 Time:	Rep 4 Time:	Rep 5 Time:
Reload Time:	Reload Time:	Reload Time:	Reload Time:	Reload Time:
A Box: Go / No Go	A Box: Go / No Go	A Box: Go / No Go	A Box: Go / No Go	A Box: Go / No Go
# of Shots::	# of Shots:	# of Shots:	# of Shots:	# of Shots:
Ave Reload Time:		**Ave Total Rep Time:**		Notes:

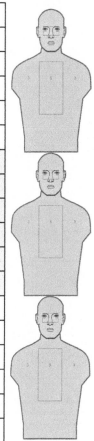

GET THAT PISTOL LOADED QUICKLY

Date:	Location:	Weapon:	Sights:	A Box: Head / Body
Rep 1 Time:	Rep 2 Time:	Rep 3 Time:	Rep 4 Time:	Rep 5 Time:
Reload Time:	Reload Time:	Reload Time:	Reload Time:	Reload Time:
A Box: Go / No Go	A Box: Go / No Go	A Box: Go / No Go	A Box: Go / No Go	A Box: Go / No Go
# of Shots:	# of Shots:	# of Shots:	# of Shots:	# of Shots:
Ave Reload Time:		**Ave Total Rep Time:**		Notes:
Date:	Location:	Weapon:	Sights:	A Box: Head / Body
Rep 1 Time:	Rep 2 Time:	Rep 3 Time:	Rep 4 Time:	Rep 5 Time:
Reload Time:	Reload Time:	Reload Time:	Reload Time:	Reload Time:
A Box: Go / No Go	A Box: Go / No Go	A Box: Go / No Go	A Box: Go / No Go	A Box: Go / No Go
# of Shots:	# of Shots:	# of Shots:	# of Shots:	# of Shots:
Ave Reload Time:		**Ave Total Rep Time:**		Notes:
Date:	Location:	Weapon:	Sights:	A Box: Head / Body
Rep 1 Time:	Rep 2 Time:	Rep 3 Time:	Rep 4 Time:	Rep 5 Time:
Reload Time:	Reload Time:	Reload Time:	Reload Time:	Reload Time:
A Box: Go / No Go	A Box: Go / No Go	A Box: Go / No Go	A Box: Go / No Go	A Box: Go / No Go
# of Shots::	# of Shots:	# of Shots:	# of Shots:	# of Shots:
Ave Reload Time:		**Ave Total Rep Time:**		Notes:

GET THAT PISTOL LOADED QUICKLY

Date:	Location:	Weapon:	Sights:	A Box: Head / Body
Rep 1 Time:	Rep 2 Time:	Rep 3 Time:	Rep 4 Time:	Rep 5 Time:
Reload Time:	Reload Time:	Reload Time:	Reload Time:	Reload Time:
A Box: Go / No Go	A Box: Go / No Go	A Box: Go / No Go	A Box: Go / No Go	A Box: Go / No Go
# of Shots:	# of Shots:	# of Shots:	# of Shots:	# of Shots:
Ave Reload Time:		**Ave Total Rep Time:**		Notes:
Date:	Location:	Weapon:	Sights:	A Box: Head / Body
Rep 1 Time:	Rep 2 Time:	Rep 3 Time:	Rep 4 Time:	Rep 5 Time:
Reload Time:	Reload Time:	Reload Time:	Reload Time:	Reload Time:
A Box: Go / No Go	A Box: Go / No Go	A Box: Go / No Go	A Box: Go / No Go	A Box: Go / No Go
# of Shots:	# of Shots:	# of Shots:	# of Shots:	# of Shots:
Ave Reload Time:		**Ave Total Rep Time:**		Notes:
Date:	Location:	Weapon:	Sights:	A Box: Head / Body
Rep 1 Time:	Rep 2 Time:	Rep 3 Time:	Rep 4 Time:	Rep 5 Time:
Reload Time:	Reload Time:	Reload Time:	Reload Time:	Reload Time:
A Box: Go / No Go	A Box: Go / No Go	A Box: Go / No Go	A Box: Go / No Go	A Box: Go / No Go
# of Shots::	# of Shots:	# of Shots:	# of Shots:	# of Shots:
Ave Reload Time:		**Ave Total Rep Time:**		Notes:

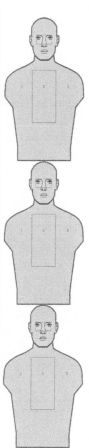

THE RACK

Purpose: Increase type 1 malfunction clearance speed and recoil management.

Distance: 10 Yards.

Target: JD-QUAL1

Extra Equipment Needed: Shot timer.

Rounds Fired Per Rep: 2 to 5 Rounds.   **Total Rounds Fired:** 10 to 25 Rounds.

Point Penalty: Go / No Go.

Repetitions: 5 Reps.

Starting Position & Condition: Standing - Pistol pointed at target with pistol in Type 1 malfunction condition (weapon condition 3, weapon cocked).

Description: At the timer beep, press the trigger and attempt to fire. Hearing the click, tap the bottom of the magazine to seat it, then rack the slide chambering a new round, aim and fire 2 to 5 rounds into the A Zone (5 point) body or A Zone (5 point) head box. Record the total time and the first shot split time. Repeat 4 more times firing the same number of rounds after clearing the malfunction as the previous repetitions. Remove the high and low times and average the 3 remaining times. If all rounds impact in the A Zone (5 point) body or head box, mark as a Go. If any rounds are shot out of the A Zone (5 point) body or head box, mark as a No Go.

Goals: Novice: 4 Seconds.   Expert: 3 Seconds.   Gunfighter: 2 Seconds.

Variations: Try different round counts on different sessions and over time, see if your average the same round counts are coming down.

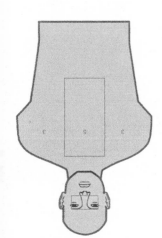

THE RACK

Date:	Location:	Weapon:	Sights:	A Box: Head / Body
Rep 1 Time:	Rep 2 Time:	Rep 3 Time:	Rep 4 Time:	Rep 5 Time:
1st Shot Time:	1st Shot Time:	1st Shot Time:	1st Shot Time:	1st Shot Time:
A Box: Go / No Go	A Box: Go / No Go	A Box: Go / No Go	A Box: Go / No Go	A Box: Go / No Go
# of Shots:	# of Shots:	# of Shots:	# of Shots:	# of Shots:
Ave 1st Shot Time:		**Ave Total Rep Time:**		Notes:
Date:	Location:	Weapon:	Sights:	A Box: Head / Body
Rep 1 Time:	Rep 2 Time:	Rep 3 Time:	Rep 4 Time:	Rep 5 Time:
1st Shot Time:	1st Shot Time:	1st Shot Time:	1st Shot Time:	1st Shot Time:
A Box: Go / No Go	A Box: Go / No Go	A Box: Go / No Go	A Box: Go / No Go	A Box: Go / No Go
# of Shots:	# of Shots:	# of Shots:	# of Shots:	# of Shots:
Ave 1st Shot Time:		**Ave Total Rep Time:**		Notes:
Date:	Location:	Weapon:	Sights:	A Box: Head / Body
Rep 1 Time:	Rep 2 Time:	Rep 3 Time:	Rep 4 Time:	Rep 5 Time:
1st Shot Time:	1st Shot Time:	1st Shot Time:	1st Shot Time:	1st Shot Time:
A Box: Go / No Go	A Box: Go / No Go	A Box: Go / No Go	A Box: Go / No Go	A Box: Go / No Go
# of Shots:	# of Shots:	# of Shots:	# of Shots:	# of Shots:
Ave 1st Shot Time:		**Ave Total Rep Time:**		Notes:

THE RACK

Date:	Location:	Weapon:	Sights:	A Box: Head / Body
Rep 1 Time:	Rep 2 Time:	Rep 3 Time:	Rep 4 Time:	Rep 5 Time:
1st Shot Time:	1st Shot Time:	1st Shot Time:	1st Shot Time:	1st Shot Time:
A Box: Go / No Go	A Box: Go / No Go	A Box: Go / No Go	A Box: Go / No Go	A Box: Go / No Go
# of Shots:	# of Shots:	# of Shots:	# of Shots:	# of Shots:
Ave 1st Shot Time:		**Ave Total Rep Time:**		Notes:

Date:	Location:	Weapon:	Sights:	A Box: Head / Body
Rep 1 Time:	Rep 2 Time:	Rep 3 Time:	Rep 4 Time:	Rep 5 Time:
1st Shot Time:	1st Shot Time:	1st Shot Time:	1st Shot Time:	1st Shot Time:
A Box: Go / No Go	A Box: Go / No Go	A Box: Go / No Go	A Box: Go / No Go	A Box: Go / No Go
# of Shots:	# of Shots:	# of Shots:	# of Shots:	# of Shots:
Ave 1st Shot Time:		**Ave Total Rep Time:**		Notes:

Date:	Location:	Weapon:	Sights:	A Box: Head / Body
Rep 1 Time:	Rep 2 Time:	Rep 3 Time:	Rep 4 Time:	Rep 5 Time:
1st Shot Time:	1st Shot Time:	1st Shot Time:	1st Shot Time:	1st Shot Time:
A Box: Go / No Go	A Box: Go / No Go	A Box: Go / No Go	A Box: Go / No Go	A Box: Go / No Go
# of Shots:	# of Shots:	# of Shots:	# of Shots:	# of Shots:
Ave 1st Shot Time:		**Ave Total Rep Time:**		Notes:

THE RACK

Date:	Location:	Weapon:	Sights:	A Box: Head / Body
Rep 1 Time:	Rep 2 Time:	Rep 3 Time:	Rep 4 Time:	Rep 5 Time:
1st Shot Time:	1st Shot Time:	1st Shot Time:	1st Shot Time:	1st Shot Time:
A Box: Go / No Go	A Box: Go / No Go	A Box: Go / No Go	A Box: Go / No Go	A Box: Go / No Go
# of Shots:	# of Shots:	# of Shots:	# of Shots:	# of Shots:
Ave 1st Shot Time:		**Ave Total Rep Time:**		Notes:
Date:	Location:	Weapon:	Sights:	A Box: Head / Body
Rep 1 Time:	Rep 2 Time:	Rep 3 Time:	Rep 4 Time:	Rep 5 Time:
1st Shot Time:	1st Shot Time:	1st Shot Time:	1st Shot Time:	1st Shot Time:
A Box: Go / No Go	A Box: Go / No Go	A Box: Go / No Go	A Box: Go / No Go	A Box: Go / No Go
# of Shots:	# of Shots:	# of Shots:	# of Shots:	# of Shots:
Ave 1st Shot Time:		**Ave Total Rep Time:**		Notes:
Date:	Location:	Weapon:	Sights:	A Box: Head / Body
Rep 1 Time:	Rep 2 Time:	Rep 3 Time:	Rep 4 Time:	Rep 5 Time:
1st Shot Time:	1st Shot Time:	1st Shot Time:	1st Shot Time:	1st Shot Time:
A Box: Go / No Go	A Box: Go / No Go	A Box: Go / No Go	A Box: Go / No Go	A Box: Go / No Go
# of Shots:	# of Shots:	# of Shots:	# of Shots:	# of Shots:
Ave 1st Shot Time:		**Ave Total Rep Time:**		Notes:

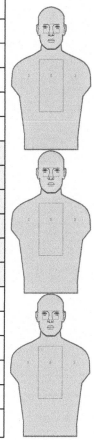

Manipulation Drills - 4

THE RACK

Date:	Location:	Weapon:	Sights:	A Box: Head / Body
Rep 1 Time:	Rep 2 Time:	Rep 3 Time:	Rep 4 Time:	Rep 5 Time:
1st Shot Time:	1st Shot Time:	1st Shot Time:	1st Shot Time:	1st Shot Time:
A Box: Go / No Go	A Box: Go / No Go	A Box: Go / No Go	A Box: Go / No Go	A Box: Go / No Go
# of Shots:	# of Shots:	# of Shots:	# of Shots:	# of Shots:
Ave 1st Shot Time:		**Ave Total Rep Time:**		Notes:
Date:	Location:	Weapon:	Sights:	A Box: Head / Body
Rep 1 Time:	Rep 2 Time:	Rep 3 Time:	Rep 4 Time:	Rep 5 Time:
1st Shot Time:	1st Shot Time:	1st Shot Time:	1st Shot Time:	1st Shot Time:
A Box: Go / No Go	A Box: Go / No Go	A Box: Go / No Go	A Box: Go / No Go	A Box: Go / No Go
# of Shots:	# of Shots:	# of Shots:	# of Shots:	# of Shots:
Ave 1st Shot Time:		**Ave Total Rep Time:**		Notes:
Date:	Location:	Weapon:	Sights:	A Box: Head / Body
Rep 1 Time:	Rep 2 Time:	Rep 3 Time:	Rep 4 Time:	Rep 5 Time:
1st Shot Time:	1st Shot Time:	1st Shot Time:	1st Shot Time:	1st Shot Time:
A Box: Go / No Go	A Box: Go / No Go	A Box: Go / No Go	A Box: Go / No Go	A Box: Go / No Go
# of Shots:	# of Shots:	# of Shots:	# of Shots:	# of Shots:
Ave 1st Shot Time:		**Ave Total Rep Time:**		Notes:

THE RACK

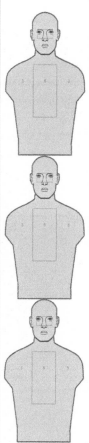

Date:	Location:	Weapon:	Sights:	A Box: Head / Body
Rep 1 Time:	Rep 2 Time:	Rep 3 Time:	Rep 4 Time:	Rep 5 Time:
1st Shot Time:	1st Shot Time:	1st Shot Time:	1st Shot Time:	1st Shot Time:
A Box: Go / No Go	A Box: Go / No Go	A Box: Go / No Go	A Box: Go / No Go	A Box: Go / No Go
# of Shots:	# of Shots:	# of Shots:	# of Shots:	# of Shots:
Ave 1st Shot Time:		**Ave Total Rep Time:**		Notes:
Date:	Location:	Weapon:	Sights:	A Box: Head / Body
Rep 1 Time:	Rep 2 Time:	Rep 3 Time:	Rep 4 Time:	Rep 5 Time:
1st Shot Time:	1st Shot Time:	1st Shot Time:	1st Shot Time:	1st Shot Time:
A Box: Go / No Go	A Box: Go / No Go	A Box: Go / No Go	A Box: Go / No Go	A Box: Go / No Go
# of Shots:	# of Shots:	# of Shots:	# of Shots:	# of Shots:
Ave 1st Shot Time:		**Ave Total Rep Time:**		Notes:
Date:	Location:	Weapon:	Sights:	A Box: Head / Body
Rep 1 Time:	Rep 2 Time:	Rep 3 Time:	Rep 4 Time:	Rep 5 Time:
1st Shot Time:	1st Shot Time:	1st Shot Time:	1st Shot Time:	1st Shot Time:
A Box: Go / No Go	A Box: Go / No Go	A Box: Go / No Go	A Box: Go / No Go	A Box: Go / No Go
# of Shots:	# of Shots:	# of Shots:	# of Shots:	# of Shots:
Ave 1st Shot Time:		**Ave Total Rep Time:**		Notes:

DOUBLE UP

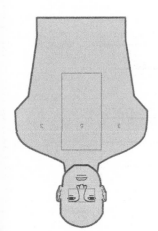

Purpose: Increase type 2 malfunction clearance speed.

Distance: 10 Yards.

Target: JD-QUAL1

Extra Equipment Needed: Shot timer, 2 magazines, 1 magazine pouch

Rounds Fired Per Rep: 2 to 5 Rounds.   **Total Rounds Fired:** 10 to 25 Rounds.

Point Penalty: As per target score.

Repetitions: 5 Reps.

Starting Position & Condition: Standing - Pistol pointed at target with pistol put in a Type 2 (double feed) malfunction condition.

Description: Pistol pointed at target, at the timer beep, press the trigger and attempt to fire. Hearing no click and feeling a mushy trigger; tilt the pistol up and observe the chamber. Upon seeing the double feed, rack the slide and lock it back. Remove the magazine that is in the pistol and let it drop on the ground. Rack the slide 3 times or until you see the stuck round/case in the chamber extracted. Bring the pistol up in front of your face with your hand just below your eyes so you can still see what's going on in front of you and with your elbow tucked into your side, take the magazine out of the magazine pouch with live rounds in it and insert it into the magazine well. After you have inserted the magazine half way; transition from the grip to the palm of your hand pushing on the bottom of the magazine. Push forcefully to the point where you hear a click of the magazine being locked in place. Rack the slide to chamber a round, aim and fire 2 to 5 rounds into the (5 point) A Zone body or (5 point) A Zone head box after reloading. Record the time. Repeat 4 more times firing the same number of rounds after clearing the malfunction as the previous repetitions. Remove the high and low times and average the 3 remaining times for an average.

Goals: To be smooth and deliberate.

DOUBLE UP

Date:	Location:	Weapon:	Sights:	A Box: Head / Body
Rep 1 Time:	Rep 2 Time:	Rep 3 Time:	Rep 4 Time:	Rep 5 Time:
1st Shot Time:	1st Shot Time:	1st Shot Time:	1st Shot Time:	1st Shot Time:
# of Shots:	# of Shots:	# of Shots:	# of Shots:	# of Shots:
Ave 1st Shot Time:		**Ave Total Rep Time:**		Notes:

Date:	Location:	Weapon:	Sights:	A Box: Head / Body
Rep 1 Time:	Rep 2 Time:	Rep 3 Time:	Rep 4 Time:	Rep 5 Time:
1st Shot Time:	1st Shot Time:	1st Shot Time:	1st Shot Time:	1st Shot Time:
# of Shots:	# of Shots:	# of Shots:	# of Shots:	# of Shots:
Ave 1st Shot Time:		**Ave Total Rep Time:**		Notes:

Date:	Location:	Weapon:	Sights:	A Box: Head / Body
Rep 1 Time:	Rep 2 Time:	Rep 3 Time:	Rep 4 Time:	Rep 5 Time:
1st Shot Time:	1st Shot Time:	1st Shot Time:	1st Shot Time:	1st Shot Time:
# of Shots::	# of Shots:	# of Shots:	# of Shots:	# of Shots:
Ave 1st Shot Time:		**Ave Total Rep Time:**		Notes:

DOUBLE UP

Date:	Location:	Weapon:	Sights:	A Box: Head / Body
Rep 1 Time:	Rep 2 Time:	Rep 3 Time:	Rep 4 Time:	Rep 5 Time:
1st Shot Time:	1st Shot Time:	1st Shot Time:	1st Shot Time:	1st Shot Time:
# of Shots:	# of Shots:	# of Shots:	# of Shots:	# of Shots:
Ave 1st Shot Time:		**Ave Total Rep Time:**		Notes:

Date:	Location:	Weapon:	Sights:	A Box: Head / Body
Rep 1 Time:	Rep 2 Time:	Rep 3 Time:	Rep 4 Time:	Rep 5 Time:
1st Shot Time:	1st Shot Time:	1st Shot Time:	1st Shot Time:	1st Shot Time:
# of Shots:	# of Shots:	# of Shots:	# of Shots:	# of Shots:
Ave 1st Shot Time:		**Ave Total Rep Time:**		Notes:

Date:	Location:	Weapon:	Sights:	A Box: Head / Body
Rep 1 Time:	Rep 2 Time:	Rep 3 Time:	Rep 4 Time:	Rep 5 Time:
1st Shot Time:	1st Shot Time:	1st Shot Time:	1st Shot Time:	1st Shot Time:
# of Shots::	# of Shots:	# of Shots:	# of Shots:	# of Shots:
Ave 1st Shot Time:		**Ave Total Rep Time:**		Notes:

DOUBLE UP

Date:	Location:	Weapon:	Sights:	A Box: Head / Body
Rep 1 Time:	Rep 2 Time:	Rep 3 Time:	Rep 4 Time:	Rep 5 Time:
1st Shot Time:	1st Shot Time:	1st Shot Time:	1st Shot Time:	1st Shot Time:
# of Shots:	# of Shots:	# of Shots:	# of Shots:	# of Shots:
Ave 1st Shot Time:		**Ave Total Rep Time:**		Notes:

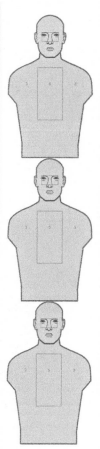

Date:	Location:	Weapon:	Sights:	A Box: Head / Body
Rep 1 Time:	Rep 2 Time:	Rep 3 Time:	Rep 4 Time:	Rep 5 Time:
1st Shot Time:	1st Shot Time:	1st Shot Time:	1st Shot Time:	1st Shot Time:
# of Shots:	# of Shots:	# of Shots:	# of Shots:	# of Shots:
Ave 1st Shot Time:		**Ave Total Rep Time:**		Notes:

Date:	Location:	Weapon:	Sights:	A Box: Head / Body
Rep 1 Time:	Rep 2 Time:	Rep 3 Time:	Rep 4 Time:	Rep 5 Time:
1st Shot Time:	1st Shot Time:	1st Shot Time:	1st Shot Time:	1st Shot Time:
# of Shots::	# of Shots:	# of Shots:	# of Shots:	# of Shots:
Ave 1st Shot Time:		**Ave Total Rep Time:**		Notes:

POWER OF 5

Purpose: Increase reloading speed, nervous system memory of an emergency reload and recoil management.

Distance: 5 Yards.

Target: JD-QUAL1

Par Time: 5.5 Seconds.

Extra Equipment Needed: Shot timer, 2 magazines, 1 magazine pouch.

Rounds Fired Per Rep: 5 Rounds.   **Total Rounds Fired:** 25 Rounds.

Point Penalty: As per target score.

Repetitions: 5 Reps.

Starting Position & Condition: Standing – Any ready position. Pistol in condition 1 with a magazine with 1 round in it.

Description: At the timer beep, fire 2 rounds into the (5 point) A Zone body box, reload the pistol, aim and fire 3 rounds into the (5 point) A Zone body or head box after reloading. Record the time and score. Repeat 4 more times. Record your score and time for reference.

Goals: Novice: 100 points in 5.5 second par time.   Expert: 120 points in 4 second par time.   Gunfighter: 125 points in 3.5 second par time.

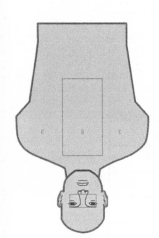

POWER OF 5

Date:	Location:	Weapon:	Sights:	A Box: Head / Body
Rep 1 Time:	Rep 2 Time:	Rep 3 Time:	Rep 4 Time:	Rep 5 Time:
Reload Time:	Reload Time:	Reload Time:	Reload Time:	Reload Time:
Rep 1 Score:	Rep 2 Score:	Rep 3 Score:	Rep 4 Score:	Rep 5 Score:
Total Rep Score:		Notes:		

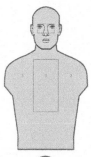

Date:	Location:	Weapon:	Sights:	A Box: Head / Body
Rep 1 Time:	Rep 2 Time:	Rep 3 Time:	Rep 4 Time:	Rep 5 Time:
Reload Time:	Reload Time:	Reload Time:	Reload Time:	Reload Time:
Rep 1 Score:	Rep 2 Score:	Rep 3 Score:	Rep 4 Score:	Rep 5 Score:
Total Rep Score:		Notes:		

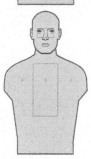

Date:	Location:	Weapon:	Sights:	A Box: Head / Body
Rep 1 Time:	Rep 2 Time:	Rep 3 Time:	Rep 4 Time:	Rep 5 Time:
Reload Time:	Reload Time:	Reload Time:	Reload Time:	Reload Time:
Rep 1 Score:	Rep 2 Score:	Rep 3 Score:	Rep 4 Score:	Rep 5 Score:
Total Rep Score:		Notes:		

POWER OF 5

Date:	Location:	Weapon:	Sights:	A Box: Head / Body
Rep 1 Time:	Rep 2 Time:	Rep 3 Time:	Rep 4 Time:	Rep 5 Time:
Reload Time:	Reload Time:	Reload Time:	Reload Time:	Reload Time:
Rep 1 Score:	Rep 2 Score:	Rep 3 Score:	Rep 4 Score:	Rep 5 Score:
Total Rep Score:		Notes:		

Date:	Location:	Weapon:	Sights:	A Box: Head / Body
Rep 1 Time:	Rep 2 Time:	Rep 3 Time:	Rep 4 Time:	Rep 5 Time:
Reload Time:	Reload Time:	Reload Time:	Reload Time:	Reload Time:
Rep 1 Score:	Rep 2 Score:	Rep 3 Score:	Rep 4 Score:	Rep 5 Score:
Total Rep Score:		Notes:		

Date:	Location:	Weapon:	Sights:	A Box: Head / Body
Rep 1 Time:	Rep 2 Time:	Rep 3 Time:	Rep 4 Time:	Rep 5 Time:
Reload Time:	Reload Time:	Reload Time:	Reload Time:	Reload Time:
Rep 1 Score:	Rep 2 Score:	Rep 3 Score:	Rep 4 Score:	Rep 5 Score:
Total Rep Score:		Notes:		

POWER OF 5

Date:	Location:	Weapon:	Sights:	A Box: Head / Body
Rep 1 Time:	Rep 2 Time:	Rep 3 Time:	Rep 4 Time:	Rep 5 Time:
Reload Time:	Reload Time:	Reload Time:	Reload Time:	Reload Time:
Rep 1 Score:	Rep 2 Score:	Rep 3 Score:	Rep 4 Score:	Rep 5 Score:
Total Rep Score:		Notes:		

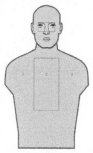

Date:	Location:	Weapon:	Sights:	A Box: Head / Body
Rep 1 Time:	Rep 2 Time:	Rep 3 Time:	Rep 4 Time:	Rep 5 Time:
Reload Time:	Reload Time:	Reload Time:	Reload Time:	Reload Time:
Rep 1 Score:	Rep 2 Score:	Rep 3 Score:	Rep 4 Score:	Rep 5 Score:
Total Rep Score:		Notes:		

Date:	Location:	Weapon:	Sights:	A Box: Head / Body
Rep 1 Time:	Rep 2 Time:	Rep 3 Time:	Rep 4 Time:	Rep 5 Time:
Reload Time:	Reload Time:	Reload Time:	Reload Time:	Reload Time:
Rep 1 Score:	Rep 2 Score:	Rep 3 Score:	Rep 4 Score:	Rep 5 Score:
Total Rep Score:		Notes:		

POWER OF 5

Date:	Location:	Weapon:	Sights:	A Box: Head / Body
Rep 1 Time:	Rep 2 Time:	Rep 3 Time:	Rep 4 Time:	Rep 5 Time:
Reload Time:	Reload Time:	Reload Time:	Reload Time:	Reload Time:
Rep 1 Score:	Rep 2 Score:	Rep 3 Score:	Rep 4 Score:	Rep 5 Score:
Total Rep Score:			Notes:	

Date:	Location:	Weapon:	Sights:	A Box: Head / Body
Rep 1 Time:	Rep 2 Time:	Rep 3 Time:	Rep 4 Time:	Rep 5 Time:
Reload Time:	Reload Time:	Reload Time:	Reload Time:	Reload Time:
Rep 1 Score:	Rep 2 Score:	Rep 3 Score:	Rep 4 Score:	Rep 5 Score:
Total Rep Score:			Notes:	

Date:	Location:	Weapon:	Sights:	A Box: Head / Body
Rep 1 Time:	Rep 2 Time:	Rep 3 Time:	Rep 4 Time:	Rep 5 Time:
Reload Time:	Reload Time:	Reload Time:	Reload Time:	Reload Time:
Rep 1 Score:	Rep 2 Score:	Rep 3 Score:	Rep 4 Score:	Rep 5 Score:
Total Rep Score:			Notes:	

POWER OF 5

Date:	Location:	Weapon:	Sights:	A Box: Head / Body
Rep 1 Time:	Rep 2 Time:	Rep 3 Time:	Rep 4 Time:	Rep 5 Time:
Reload Time:	Reload Time:	Reload Time:	Reload Time:	Reload Time:
Rep 1 Score:	Rep 2 Score:	Rep 3 Score:	Rep 4 Score:	Rep 5 Score:
Total Rep Score:		Notes:		

Date:	Location:	Weapon:	Sights:	A Box: Head / Body
Rep 1 Time:	Rep 2 Time:	Rep 3 Time:	Rep 4 Time:	Rep 5 Time:
Reload Time:	Reload Time:	Reload Time:	Reload Time:	Reload Time:
Rep 1 Score:	Rep 2 Score:	Rep 3 Score:	Rep 4 Score:	Rep 5 Score:
Total Rep Score:		Notes:		

Date:	Location:	Weapon:	Sights:	A Box: Head / Body
Rep 1 Time:	Rep 2 Time:	Rep 3 Time:	Rep 4 Time:	Rep 5 Time:
Reload Time:	Reload Time:	Reload Time:	Reload Time:	Reload Time:
Rep 1 Score:	Rep 2 Score:	Rep 3 Score:	Rep 4 Score:	Rep 5 Score:
Total Rep Score:		Notes:		

FOLLOW IT HOME

Purpose: Develop consistent marksmanship follow through.

Distance: 3 Yards.

Target: 1.5 inch square

Par Time: N / A.

Total Rounds Fired: 0 Rounds

Repetitions: 10 Reps.

Starting Position & Condition: Standing - Pistol aimed at target. Condition 4.

Description: Aim at target and press trigger without moving the sights, keep the trigger pressed back for 5 seconds while keeping your aim on the target after you have pressed the trigger to break a dry fire shot. Watch for sight movement when you press the trigger. Rack the slide to reset and repeat 9 more times.

Variations: From the holster.

1.5 inch
Square

FOLLOW IT HOME

Date:	Location:	Weapon:	# of Reps:	From Holster ?	Notes:
				Y / N	
				Y / N	
				Y / N	
				Y / N	
				Y / N	
				Y / N	
				Y / N	
				Y / N	
				Y / N	
				Y / N	
				Y / N	
				Y / N	
				Y / N	
				Y / N	
				Y / N	
				Y / N	
				Y / N	
				Y / N	

COMMITMENT

Purpose: Develop consistent marksmanship follow through.

Distance: 5 Yards.

Target: 1.5 inch square

Par Time: N/A.

Rounds Fired Per Rep: 1 Round.   **Total Rounds Fired:** 5 Rounds.

Repetitions: 5 Reps.

Starting Position & Condition: Standing - Pistol aimed at target. Condition 1.

Description: With the pistol in weapon condition 1 with 4 rounds in the magazine, aim at target and press trigger without moving the sights. Keep the trigger pressed back for 5 seconds while keeping your aim on the target after you have pressed the trigger to break the shot. While keeping your finger on the trigger, slowly release the trigger until you hear a click. Once you hear the click, do not let out anymore slack. Make sure of your aim and fire another shot, repeating the process until you have fired all of the repetitions.

Variations: From the holster.

1.5 inch
Square

COMMITMENT

Date:	Weapon:	Sights:	Notes:	
From the holster: Y / N	Positive Trigger Reset: Y / N	All 5 shots in: Y / N		

Date:	Weapon:	Sights:	Notes:	
From the holster: Y / N	Positive Trigger Reset: Y / N	All 5 shots in: Y / N		

Date:	Weapon:	Sights:	Notes:	
From the holster: Y / N	Positive Trigger Reset: Y / N	All 5 shots in: Y / N		

Date:	Weapon:	Sights:	Notes:	
From the holster: Y / N	Positive Trigger Reset: Y / N	All 5 shots in: Y / N		

Date:	Weapon:	Sights:	Notes:	
From the holster: Y / N	Positive Trigger Reset: Y / N	All 5 shots in: Y / N		

COMMITMENT

Date:	Weapon:	Sights:	Notes:
From the holster: Y / N	Positive Trigger Reset: Y / N	All 5 shots in: Y / N	

Date:	Weapon:	Sights:	Notes:
From the holster: Y / N	Positive Trigger Reset: Y / N	All 5 shots in: Y / N	

Date:	Weapon:	Sights:	Notes:
From the holster: Y / N	Positive Trigger Reset: Y / N	All 5 shots in: Y / N	

Date:	Weapon:	Sights:	Notes:
From the holster: Y / N	Positive Trigger Reset: Y / N	All 5 shots in: Y / N	

Date:	Weapon:	Sights:	Notes:
From the holster: Y / N	Positive Trigger Reset: Y / N	All 5 shots in: Y / N	

COMMITMENT

Date:	Weapon:	Sights:	Notes:	
From the holster: Y / N	Positive Trigger Reset: Y / N	All 5 shots in: Y / N		

Date:	Weapon:	Sights:	Notes:	
From the holster: Y / N	Positive Trigger Reset: Y / N	All 5 shots in: Y / N		

Date:	Weapon:	Sights:	Notes:	
From the holster: Y / N	Positive Trigger Reset: Y / N	All 5 shots in: Y / N		

Date:	Weapon:	Sights:	Notes:	
From the holster: Y / N	Positive Trigger Reset: Y / N	All 5 shots in: Y / N		

Date:	Weapon:	Sights:	Notes:	
From the holster: Y / N	Positive Trigger Reset: Y / N	All 5 shots in: Y / N		

COMMITMENT

Date:	Weapon:	Sights:	Notes:
From the holster: Y / N	Positive Trigger Reset: Y / N	All 5 shots in: Y / N	

Date:	Weapon:	Sights:	Notes:
From the holster: Y / N	Positive Trigger Reset: Y / N	All 5 shots in: Y / N	

Date:	Weapon:	Sights:	Notes:
From the holster: Y / N	Positive Trigger Reset: Y / N	All 5 shots in: Y / N	

Date:	Weapon:	Sights:	Notes:
From the holster: Y / N	Positive Trigger Reset: Y / N	All 5 shots in: Y / N	

Date:	Weapon:	Sights:	Notes:
From the holster: Y / N	Positive Trigger Reset: Y / N	All 5 shots in: Y / N	

COMMITMENT

Date:	Weapon:	Sights:	Notes:
From the holster: Y / N	Positive Trigger Reset: Y / N	All 5 shots in: Y / N	

Date:	Weapon:	Sights:	Notes:
From the holster: Y / N	Positive Trigger Reset: Y / N	All 5 shots in: Y / N	

Date:	Weapon:	Sights:	Notes:
From the holster: Y / N	Positive Trigger Reset: Y / N	All 5 shots in: Y / N	

Date:	Weapon:	Sights:	Notes:
From the holster: Y / N	Positive Trigger Reset: Y / N	All 5 shots in: Y / N	

Date:	Weapon:	Sights:	Notes:
From the holster: Y / N	Positive Trigger Reset: Y / N	All 5 shots in: Y / N	

5 BY 5

Purpose: Decrease shot anticipation and increase accuracy.

Distance: 5 Yards.

Target: 1.5 inch squares X 5

Par Time: N / A.

Rounds Fired Per Rep: 5 Rounds. **Total Rounds Fired:** 25 Rounds.

Repetitions: 5 Reps.

Starting Position & Condition: Standing - Pistol aimed at target. Condition 1.

Description: Fire 5 rounds into a 1.5 inch square target. The goal is to get all rounds into the 1.5 inch square target. After you have fired 5 live rounds, unload the pistol and with the pistol in weapon condition 4 (No round in the chamber, no live rounds, no magazine target cocked), aim at the 1.5 inch square target and press the trigger dry firing without moving the sights for a repetition of 5 good dry fires. After you have dry fired 5 times, load the pistol and repeat the cycle of 5 live rounds and 5 dry fires for a total of 5 cycles. Taking your time and getting good accurate hits in the 1.5 inch target is the goal. The dry fires after the live fire may show that you are anticipating the shot if your pistol dips when you press the trigger, causing you to be less accurate than you could be.

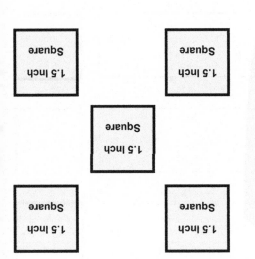

5 BY 5 DRILL

Date:	Weapon:	Sights:	Notes:	
1st group all in: Y / N	2nd group all in: Y / N	3rd group all in: Y / N	4th group all in: Y / N	5th group all in: Y / N

Date:	Weapon:	Sights:	Notes:	
1st group all in: Y / N	2nd group all in: Y / N	3rd group all in: Y / N	4th group all in: Y / N	5th group all in: Y / N

Date:	Weapon:	Sights:	Notes:	
1st group all in: Y / N	2nd group all in: Y / N	3rd group all in: Y / N	4th group all in: Y / N	5th group all in: Y / N

Date:	Weapon:	Sights:	Notes:	
1st group all in: Y / N	2nd group all in: Y / N	3rd group all in: Y / N	4th group all in: Y / N	5th group all in: Y / N

Date:	Weapon:	Sights:	Notes:	
1st group all in: Y / N	2nd group all in: Y / N	3rd group all in: Y / N	4th group all in: Y / N	5th group all in: Y / N

5 BY 5 DRILL

Date:	Weapon:	Sights:	Notes:	
1st group all in: Y / N	2nd group all in: Y / N	3rd group all in: Y / N	4th group all in: Y / N	5th group all in: Y / N

Date:	Weapon:	Sights:	Notes:	
1st group all in: Y / N	2nd group all in: Y / N	3rd group all in: Y / N	4th group all in: Y / N	5th group all in: Y / N

Date:	Weapon:	Sights:	Notes:	
1st group all in: Y / N	2nd group all in: Y / N	3rd group all in: Y / N	4th group all in: Y / N	5th group all in: Y / N

Date:	Weapon:	Sights:	Notes:	
1st group all in: Y / N	2nd group all in: Y / N	3rd group all in: Y / N	4th group all in: Y / N	5th group all in: Y / N

Date:	Weapon:	Sights:	Notes:	
1st group all in: Y / N	2nd group all in: Y / N	3rd group all in: Y / N	4th group all in: Y / N	5th group all in: Y / N

5 BY 5 DRILL

Date:	Weapon:	Sights:	Notes:	
1st group all in: Y / N	2nd group all in: Y / N	3rd group all in: Y / N	4th group all in: Y / N	5th group all in: Y / N

Date:	Weapon:	Sights:	Notes:	
1st group all in: Y / N	2nd group all in: Y / N	3rd group all in: Y / N	4th group all in: Y / N	5th group all in: Y / N

Date:	Weapon:	Sights:	Notes:	
1st group all in: Y / N	2nd group all in: Y / N	3rd group all in: Y / N	4th group all in: Y / N	5th group all in: Y / N

Date:	Weapon:	Sights:	Notes:	
1st group all in: Y / N	2nd group all in: Y / N	3rd group all in: Y / N	4th group all in: Y / N	5th group all in: Y / N

Date:	Weapon:	Sights:	Notes:	
1st group all in: Y / N	2nd group all in: Y / N	3rd group all in: Y / N	4th group all in: Y / N	5th group all in: Y / N

5 BY 5 DRILL

Date:	Weapon:	Sights:	Notes:
1st group all in: Y / N	2nd group all in: Y / N	3rd group all in: Y / N	4th group all in: Y / N	5th group all in: Y / N

Date:	Weapon:	Sights:	Notes:
1st group all in: Y / N	2nd group all in: Y / N	3rd group all in: Y / N	4th group all in: Y / N	5th group all in: Y / N

Date:	Weapon:	Sights:	Notes:
1st group all in: Y / N	2nd group all in: Y / N	3rd group all in: Y / N	4th group all in: Y / N	5th group all in: Y / N

Date:	Weapon:	Sights:	Notes:
1st group all in: Y / N	2nd group all in: Y / N	3rd group all in: Y / N	4th group all in: Y / N	5th group all in: Y / N

Date:	Weapon:	Sights:	Notes:
1st group all in: Y / N	2nd group all in: Y / N	3rd group all in: Y / N	4th group all in: Y / N	5th group all in: Y / N

5 BY 5 DRILL

Date:	Weapon:	Sights:	Notes:	
1st group all in: Y / N	2nd group all in: Y / N	3rd group all in: Y / N	4th group all in: Y / N	5th group all in: Y / N

Date:	Weapon:	Sights:	Notes:	
1st group all in: Y / N	2nd group all in: Y / N	3rd group all in: Y / N	4th group all in: Y / N	5th group all in: Y / N

Date:	Weapon:	Sights:	Notes:	
1st group all in: Y / N	2nd group all in: Y / N	3rd group all in: Y / N	4th group all in: Y / N	5th group all in: Y / N

Date:	Weapon:	Sights:	Notes:	
1st group all in: Y / N	2nd group all in: Y / N	3rd group all in: Y / N	4th group all in: Y / N	5th group all in: Y / N

Date:	Weapon:	Sights:	Notes:	
1st group all in: Y / N	2nd group all in: Y / N	3rd group all in: Y / N	4th group all in: Y / N	5th group all in: Y / N

STAND STEADY

Purpose: Accuracy.

Distance: 5, 7, 10, 15 and 25 Yards.

Target: GF-1

Rounds Fired Per Rep: 3 Rounds.

Point Penalty: As per target score.

Repetitions: 1 Rep.

Starting Position & Condition: Standing - Low ready. Condition 1.

Description: At your own personal go, from the low ready, raise your pistol, take a good aim and fire 3 rounds into the target from each distance of 5, 7, 10, 15 and 25 yards. The goal is to make at least 135 points. A Gunfighter score is going to be extremely hard to do, so keep working at it. Take your time and make every shot count. There is no time limit and if you feel you are going to break a bad shot, stop and start that shot over.

Goals: Novice: 135 points.   Expert: 150 Points.   Gunfighter: 150 points with 10 X's.

Total Rounds Fired: 15 Rounds.

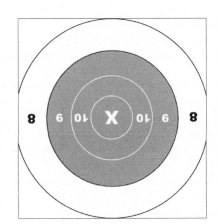

STAND STEADY

Date:	Location:	Weapon:	Ammo:
# Outside:	# of 8's:	# of 9's:	Notes:
# of 10's:	**TOTAL SCORE:**	**X's**	

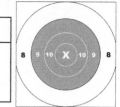

Date:	Location:	Weapon:	Ammo:
# Outside:	# of 8's:	# of 9's:	Notes:
# of 10's:	**TOTAL SCORE:**	**X's**	

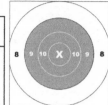

Date:	Location:	Weapon:	Ammo:
# Outside:	# of 8's:	# of 9's:	Notes:
# of 10's:	**TOTAL SCORE:**	**X's**	

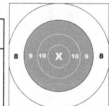

Date:	Location:	Weapon:	Ammo:
# Outside:	# of 8's:	# of 9's:	Notes:
# of 10's:	**TOTAL SCORE:**	**X's**	

STAND STEADY

Date:	Location:	Weapon:	Ammo:
# Outside:	# of 8's:	# of 9's:	Notes:
# of 10's:	**TOTAL SCORE:**	X's	

Date:	Location:	Weapon:	Ammo:
# Outside:	# of 8's:	# of 9's:	Notes:
# of 10's:	**TOTAL SCORE:**	X's	

Date:	Location:	Weapon:	Ammo:
# Outside:	# of 8's:	# of 9's:	Notes:
# of 10's:	**TOTAL SCORE:**	X's	

Date:	Location:	Weapon:	Ammo:
# Outside:	# of 8's:	# of 9's:	Notes:
# of 10's:	**TOTAL SCORE:**	X's	

STAND STEADY

Date:	Location:	Weapon:	Ammo:
# Outside:	# of 8's:	# of 9's:	Notes:
# of 10's:	**TOTAL SCORE:**	**X's**	

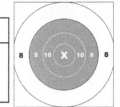

Date:	Location:	Weapon:	Ammo:
# Outside:	# of 8's:	# of 9's:	Notes:
# of 10's:	**TOTAL SCORE:**	**X's**	

Date:	Location:	Weapon:	Ammo:
# Outside:	# of 8's:	# of 9's:	Notes:
# of 10's:	**TOTAL SCORE:**	**X's**	

Date:	Location:	Weapon:	Ammo:
# Outside:	# of 8's:	# of 9's:	Notes:
# of 10's:	**TOTAL SCORE:**	**X's**	

Card 1

# of 10's:	TOTAL SCORE:	X's:	
# Outside:	# of 8's:	# of 9's:	Notes:
Date:	Location:	Weapon:	Ammo:

Card 2

# of 10's:	TOTAL SCORE:	X's:	
# Outside:	# of 8's:	# of 9's:	Notes:
Date:	Location:	Weapon:	Ammo:

Card 3

# of 10's:	TOTAL SCORE:	X's:	
# Outside:	# of 8's:	# of 9's:	Notes:
Date:	Location:	Weapon:	Ammo:

Card 4

# of 10's:	TOTAL SCORE:	X's:	
# Outside:	# of 8's:	# of 9's:	Notes:
Date:	Location:	Weapon:	Ammo:

STAND STEADY

Date:	Location:	Weapon:	Ammo:
# Outside:	# of 8's:	# of 9's:	Notes:
# of 10's:	**TOTAL SCORE:**	**X's**	

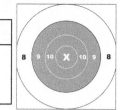

Date:	Location:	Weapon:	Ammo:
# Outside:	# of 8's:	# of 9's:	Notes:
# of 10's:	**TOTAL SCORE:**	**X's**	

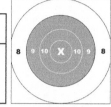

Date:	Location:	Weapon:	Ammo:
# Outside:	# of 8's:	# of 9's:	Notes:
# of 10's:	**TOTAL SCORE:**	**X's**	

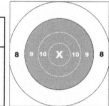

Date:	Location:	Weapon:	Ammo:
# Outside:	# of 8's:	# of 9's:	Notes:
# of 10's:	**TOTAL SCORE:**	**X's**	

VERSATILE

Purpose: Accuracy with different shooting styles.

Distance: 10 Yards.

Target: JD-QUAL1

Par Time: N / A.

Rounds Fired Per Rep: 5 Rounds.   **Total Rounds Fired:** 20 Rounds.

Point penalty: As per target score.

Starting Position & Condition: Standing - Low ready. Condition 1.

Description: Aim and fire 5 rounds into the (5 point) A Zone body box. After you are done firing all of the 4 stages, record your score.

- Stage 1 – Fire 5 rounds dominant hand (two handed).
- Stage 2 – Fire 5 rounds dominant hand (one handed).
- Stage 3 – Fire 5 rounds non-dominant hand (one handed).
- Stage 4 – Fire 5 rounds non-dominant hand (two handed).

Goals: Novice: All shots in body.   Expert: All shots in body A box.   Gunfighter: All shots in head A box from 15 yards.

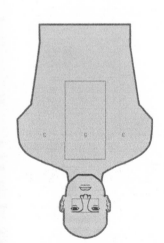

VERSATILE

Date:	Location:	Weapon:	Notes:	
Stage 1 Score:	Stage 2 Score:	Stage 3 Score:	Stage 4 Score:	**Total Score:**

Date:	Location:	Weapon:	Notes:	
Stage 1 Score:	Stage 2 Score:	Stage 3 Score:	Stage 4 Score:	**Total Score:**

Date:	Location:	Weapon:	Notes:	
Stage 1 Score:	Stage 2 Score:	Stage 3 Score:	Stage 4 Score:	**Total Score:**

Date:	Location:	Weapon:	Notes:	
Stage 1 Score:	Stage 2 Score:	Stage 3 Score:	Stage 4 Score:	**Total Score:**

Date:	Location:	Weapon:	Notes:	
Stage 1 Score:	Stage 2 Score:	Stage 3 Score:	Stage 4 Score:	Total Score:

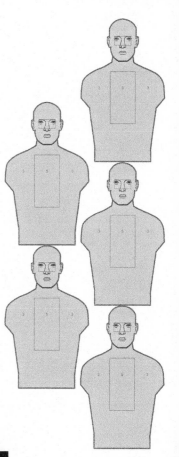

VERSATILE

Date:	Location:	Weapon:	Notes:
Stage 1 Score:	Stage 2 Score:	Stage 3 Score:	Stage 4 Score:	Total Score:

Date:	Location:	Weapon:	Notes:
Stage 1 Score:	Stage 2 Score:	Stage 3 Score:	Stage 4 Score:	Total Score:

Date:	Location:	Weapon:	Notes:
Stage 1 Score:	Stage 2 Score:	Stage 3 Score:	Stage 4 Score:	Total Score:

Date:	Location:	Weapon:	Notes:
Stage 1 Score:	Stage 2 Score:	Stage 3 Score:	Stage 4 Score:	Total Score:

Date:	Location:	Weapon:	Notes:
Stage 1 Score:	Stage 2 Score:	Stage 3 Score:	Stage 4 Score:	Total Score:

VERSATILE

Date:	Location:	Weapon:	Notes:	
Stage 1 Score:	Stage 2 Score:	Stage 3 Score:	Stage 4 Score:	**Total Score:**

Date:	Location:	Weapon:	Notes:	
Stage 1 Score:	Stage 2 Score:	Stage 3 Score:	Stage 4 Score:	**Total Score:**

Date:	Location:	Weapon:	Notes:	
Stage 1 Score:	Stage 2 Score:	Stage 3 Score:	Stage 4 Score:	**Total Score:**

Date:	Location:	Weapon:	Notes:	
Stage 1 Score:	Stage 2 Score:	Stage 3 Score:	Stage 4 Score:	**Total Score:**

Date:	Location:	Weapon:	Notes:	
Stage 1 Score:	Stage 2 Score:	Stage 3 Score:	Stage 4 Score:	Total Score:

Date:	Location:	Weapon:	Notes:
Stage 1 Score:	Stage 2 Score:	Stage 3 Score:	Stage 4 Score:	**Total Score:**

Date:	Location:	Weapon:	Notes:
Stage 1 Score:	Stage 2 Score:	Stage 3 Score:	Stage 4 Score:	**Total Score:**

Date:	Location:	Weapon:	Notes:
Stage 1 Score:	Stage 2 Score:	Stage 3 Score:	Stage 4 Score:	**Total Score:**

Date:	Location:	Weapon:	Notes:
Stage 1 Score:	Stage 2 Score:	Stage 3 Score:	Stage 4 Score:	**Total Score:**

Date:	Location:	Weapon:	Notes:
Stage 1 Score:	Stage 2 Score:	Stage 3 Score:	Stage 4 Score:	Total Score:

VERSATILE

Date:	Location:	Weapon:	Notes:	
Stage 1 Score:	Stage 2 Score:	Stage 3 Score:	Stage 4 Score:	**Total Score:**

Date:	Location:	Weapon:	Notes:	
Stage 1 Score:	Stage 2 Score:	Stage 3 Score:	Stage 4 Score:	**Total Score:**

Date:	Location:	Weapon:	Notes:	
Stage 1 Score:	Stage 2 Score:	Stage 3 Score:	Stage 4 Score:	**Total Score:**

Date:	Location:	Weapon:	Notes:	
Stage 1 Score:	Stage 2 Score:	Stage 3 Score:	Stage 4 Score:	**Total Score:**

Date:	Location:	Weapon:	Notes:	
Stage 1 Score:	Stage 2 Score:	Stage 3 Score:	Stage 4 Score:	Total Score:

RIDE ALONG

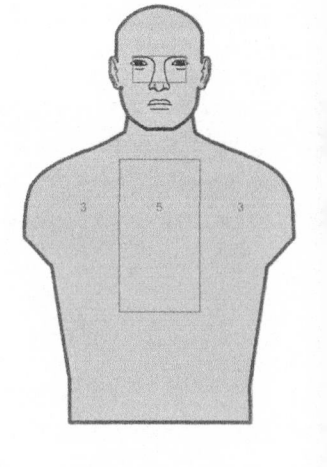

Purpose: Accuracy with one handed shooting.

Distance: 10 Yards.

Target: JD-QUAL1

Extra Equipment Needed: Shot timer.

Rounds Fired Per Stage: 5 Rounds.   **Total Rounds Fired:** 20 Rounds.

Point penalty: As per target score.

Starting Position & Condition: Standing - Low ready. Condition 1.

Description: From the one handed low ready position and your pistol in weapon condition 1 with 4 rounds in the magazine, aim and fire 3 rounds into the (5 point) A Zone body box and 2 rounds into the A Zone (5 point) head box. After you are done firing all of the 4 stages, record your score. For more advanced shooters, record your time and add 2 seconds for each round out of the A Zone boxes and 5 seconds for each round out of the A Zone boxes.

- Stage 1 – Fire 5 rounds dominant hand (one handed).

- Stage 2 – Fire 5 rounds non-dominant hand (one handed).

- Stage 3 – Fire 5 rounds dominant hand (one handed).

- Stage 4 – Fire 5 rounds non-dominant hand (one handed).

Goals: Novice: All shots in silhouette.   Expert: 86 points.   Gunfighter: 96 points or higher.

RIDE ALONG

Date:	Location:	Weapon:	Notes:	
Stage 1 Score:	Stage 2 Score:	Stage 3 Score:	Stage 4 Score:	**Total Score:**
				Time:

Date:	Location:	Weapon:	Notes:	
Stage 1 Score:	Stage 2 Score:	Stage 3 Score:	Stage 4 Score:	**Total Score:**
				Time:

Date:	Location:	Weapon:	Notes:	
Stage 1 Score:	Stage 2 Score:	Stage 3 Score:	Stage 4 Score:	**Total Score:**
				Time:

Date:	Location:	Weapon:	Notes:	
Stage 1 Score:	Stage 2 Score:	Stage 3 Score:	Stage 4 Score:	**Total Score:**
				Time:

Date:	Location:	Weapon:	Notes:	
Stage 1 Score:	Stage 2 Score:	Stage 3 Score:	Stage 4 Score:	Total Score:
				Time:

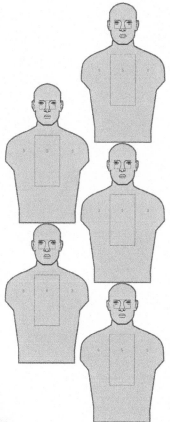

RIDE ALONG

Date:	Location:	Weapon:	Notes:	
Stage 1 Score:	Stage 2 Score:	Stage 3 Score:	Stage 4 Score:	**Total Score:**
				Time:

Date:	Location:	Weapon:	Notes:	
Stage 1 Score:	Stage 2 Score:	Stage 3 Score:	Stage 4 Score:	**Total Score:**
				Time:

Date:	Location:	Weapon:	Notes:	
Stage 1 Score:	Stage 2 Score:	Stage 3 Score:	Stage 4 Score:	**Total Score:**
				Time:

Date:	Location:	Weapon:	Notes:	
Stage 1 Score:	Stage 2 Score:	Stage 3 Score:	Stage 4 Score:	**Total Score:**
				Time:

Date:	Location:	Weapon:	Notes:	
Stage 1 Score:	Stage 2 Score:	Stage 3 Score:	Stage 4 Score:	Total Score:
				Time:

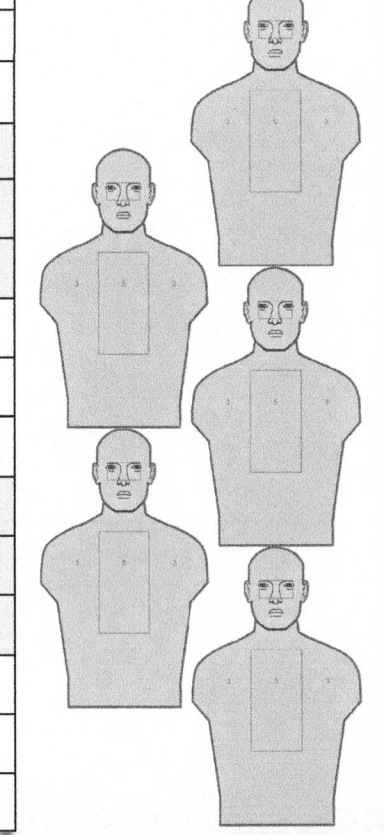

RIDE ALONG

Date:	Location:	Weapon:	Notes:	
Stage 1 Score:	Stage 2 Score:	Stage 3 Score:	Stage 4 Score:	**Total Score:**
				Time:

Date:	Location:	Weapon:	Notes:	
Stage 1 Score:	Stage 2 Score:	Stage 3 Score:	Stage 4 Score:	**Total Score:**
				Time:

Date:	Location:	Weapon:	Notes:	
Stage 1 Score:	Stage 2 Score:	Stage 3 Score:	Stage 4 Score:	**Total Score:**
				Time:

Date:	Location:	Weapon:	Notes:	
Stage 1 Score:	Stage 2 Score:	Stage 3 Score:	Stage 4 Score:	**Total Score:**
				Time:

Date:	Location:	Weapon:	Notes:	
Stage 1 Score:	Stage 2 Score:	Stage 3 Score:	Stage 4 Score:	Total Score:
				Time:

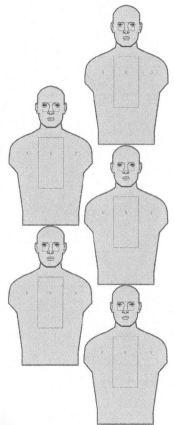

RIDE ALONG

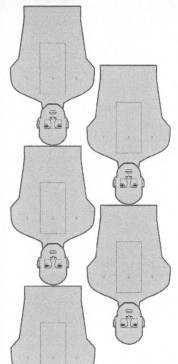
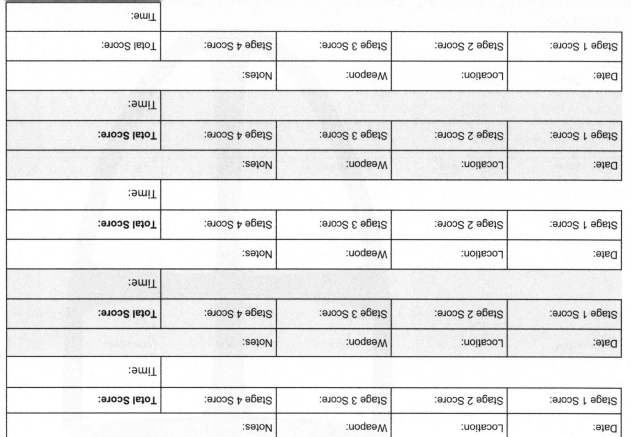

Date:	Location:	Weapon:	Notes:	
Stage 1 Score:	Stage 2 Score:	Stage 3 Score:	Stage 4 Score:	Total Score:
Time:				

Date:	Location:	Weapon:	Notes:	
Stage 1 Score:	Stage 2 Score:	Stage 3 Score:	Stage 4 Score:	Total Score:
Time:				

Date:	Location:	Weapon:	Notes:	
Stage 1 Score:	Stage 2 Score:	Stage 3 Score:	Stage 4 Score:	Total Score:
Time:				

Date:	Location:	Weapon:	Notes:	
Stage 1 Score:	Stage 2 Score:	Stage 3 Score:	Stage 4 Score:	Total Score:
Time:				

Date:	Location:	Weapon:	Notes:	
Stage 1 Score:	Stage 2 Score:	Stage 3 Score:	Stage 4 Score:	Total Score:
Time:				

RIDE ALONG

Date:	Location:	Weapon:	Notes:	
Stage 1 Score:	Stage 2 Score:	Stage 3 Score:	Stage 4 Score:	**Total Score:**
				Time:

Date:	Location:	Weapon:	Notes:	
Stage 1 Score:	Stage 2 Score:	Stage 3 Score:	Stage 4 Score:	**Total Score:**
				Time:

Date:	Location:	Weapon:	Notes:	
Stage 1 Score:	Stage 2 Score:	Stage 3 Score:	Stage 4 Score:	**Total Score:**
				Time:

Date:	Location:	Weapon:	Notes:	
Stage 1 Score:	Stage 2 Score:	Stage 3 Score:	Stage 4 Score:	**Total Score:**
				Time:

Date:	Location:	Weapon:	Notes:	
Stage 1 Score:	Stage 2 Score:	Stage 3 Score:	Stage 4 Score:	Total Score:
				Time:

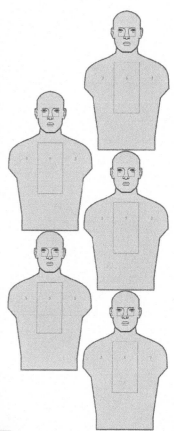

LOW READY PISTOL

Purpose: To increase competency of the use of the low ready position.

Distance: 10 Yards.

Target: JD-QUAL1

Par Time: 1 Second.

Extra Equipment Needed: Shot timer.

Rounds Fired Per Rep: 1 Round.   **Total Rounds Fired:** 5 Rounds.

Point Penalty: Go / No Go.

Repetitions: 5 Reps.

Starting Position & Condition: Standing - Low ready. Condition 1.

Description: The low ready position is where the pistols muzzle is pointed into the dirt 6 to 8 feet in front of you while you are looking at the target. From the low ready position, at the timer beep, raise the pistol and take aim at the target with a flash sight picture and fire a round within 1 second into the A Zone (5 point) body box. Record how many times you made par time and hit within the A Zone (5 point) body box.

Goals: Novice: All shots in body under par.   **Expert:** All shots in body A Zone under par.   **Gunfighter:** All shots in head A zone under par.

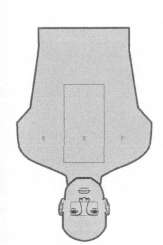

LOW READY PISTOL

Date:	Location:	Weapon:	Sights:	Notes:
A Zone: Body / Head	# Under Par:	# In A Box:	**Go / No Go**	

Date:	Location:	Weapon:	Sights:	Notes:
A Zone: Body / Head	# Under Par:	# In A Box:	**Go / No Go**	

Date:	Location:	Weapon:	Sights:	Notes:
A Zone: Body / Head	# Under Par:	# In A Box:	**Go / No Go**	

Date:	Location:	Weapon:	Sights:	Notes:
A Zone: Body / Head	# Under Par:	# In A Box:	**Go / No Go**	

Date:	Location:	Weapon:	Sights:	Notes:
A Zone: Body / Head	# Under Par:	# In A Box:	**Go / No Go**	

Ready Positions - 1

Date:	Location:	Weapon:	Sights:	Notes:
A Zone: Body / Head	# Under Par:	# In A Box:	Go / No Go	

Date:	Location:	Weapon:	Sights:	Notes:
A Zone: Body / Head	# Under Par:	# In A Box:	Go / No Go	

Date:	Location:	Weapon:	Sights:	Notes:
A Zone: Body / Head	# Under Par:	# In A Box:	Go / No Go	

Date:	Location:	Weapon:	Sights:	Notes:
A Zone: Body / Head	# Under Par:	# In A Box:	Go / No Go	

Date:	Location:	Weapon:	Sights:	Notes:
A Zone: Body / Head	# Under Par:	# In A Box:	Go / No Go	

LOW READY PISTOL

Date:	Location:	Weapon:	Sights:	Notes:
A Zone: Body / Head	# Under Par:	# In A Box:	**Go / No Go**	

Date:	Location:	Weapon:	Sights:	Notes:
A Zone: Body / Head	# Under Par:	# In A Box:	**Go / No Go**	

Date:	Location:	Weapon:	Sights:	Notes:
A Zone: Body / Head	# Under Par:	# In A Box:	**Go / No Go**	

Date:	Location:	Weapon:	Sights:	Notes:
A Zone: Body / Head	# Under Par:	# In A Box:	**Go / No Go**	

Date:	Location:	Weapon:	Sights:	Notes:
A Zone: Body / Head	# Under Par:	# In A Box:	**Go / No Go**	

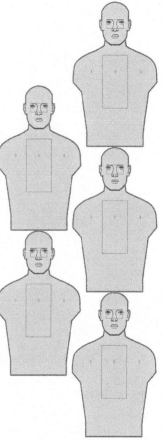

LOW READY PISTOL

Date:	A Zone: Body / Head	# Under Par:	# In A Box:	Go / No Go
Location:	Weapon:	Sights:	Notes:	

Date:	A Zone: Body / Head	# Under Par:	# In A Box:	Go / No Go
Location:	Weapon:	Sights:	Notes:	

Date:	A Zone: Body / Head	# Under Par:	# In A Box:	Go / No Go
Location:	Weapon:	Sights:	Notes:	

Date:	A Zone: Body / Head	# Under Par:	# In A Box:	Go / No Go
Location:	Weapon:	Sights:	Notes:	

Date:	A Zone: Body / Head	# Under Par:	# In A Box:	Go / No Go
Location:	Weapon:	Sights:	Notes:	

LOW READY PISTOL

Date:	Location:	Weapon:	Sights:	Notes:
A Zone: Body / Head	# Under Par:	# In A Box:	**Go / No Go**	

Date:	Location:	Weapon:	Sights:	Notes:
A Zone: Body / Head	# Under Par:	# In A Box:	**Go / No Go**	

Date:	Location:	Weapon:	Sights:	Notes:
A Zone: Body / Head	# Under Par:	# In A Box:	**Go / No Go**	

Date:	Location:	Weapon:	Sights:	Notes:
A Zone: Body / Head	# Under Par:	# In A Box:	**Go / No Go**	

Date:	Location:	Weapon:	Sights:	Notes:
A Zone: Body / Head	# Under Par:	# In A Box:	**Go / No Go**	

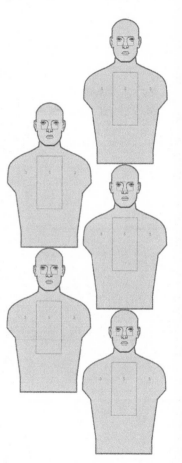

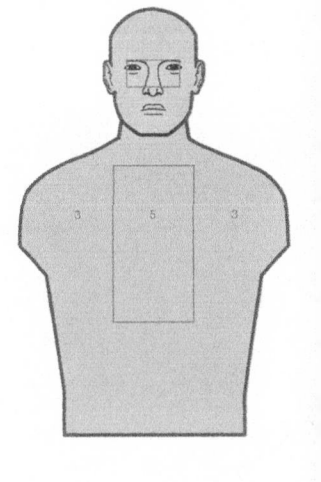

READY PISTOL

Purpose: To increase competency of the use of the ready position.

Distance: 10 Yards.

Target: JD-QUAL1

Par Time: 0.8 Second.

Extra Equipment Needed: Timer.

Rounds Fired Per Rep: 1 Round.   **Total Rounds Fired:** 5 Rounds.

Point Penalty: Go / No Go.

Repetitions: 5 Reps.

Starting Position & Condition: Standing - Ready. Condition 1.

Description: The ready position is where the pistols muzzle is pointed at the target while you are looking at the target just over the top of the sights. From the ready position, at the beep of the timer, raise the pistol and take aim at the target with a flash sight picture and fire a round within .8 seconds into the A Zone (5 point) body box. Record how many times you made par time and hit within the A Zone (5 point) body box.

Goals: Novice: All shots in body under par.   Expert: All shots in body A Zone under par.   Gunfighter: All shots in head A zone under par.

READY PISTOL

Date:	Location:	Weapon:	Sights:	Notes:
A Zone: Body / Head	# Under Par:	# In A Box:	**Go / No Go**	

Date:	Location:	Weapon:	Sights:	Notes:
A Zone: Body / Head	# Under Par:	# In A Box:	**Go / No Go**	

Date:	Location:	Weapon:	Sights:	Notes:
A Zone: Body / Head	# Under Par:	# In A Box:	**Go / No Go**	

Date:	Location:	Weapon:	Sights:	Notes:
A Zone: Body / Head	# Under Par:	# In A Box:	**Go / No Go**	

Date:	Location:	Weapon:	Sights:	Notes:
A Zone: Body / Head	# Under Par:	# In A Box:	**Go / No Go**	

READY PISTOL

Date:	A Zone: Body / Head	# Under Par:	# In A Box:	Go / No Go
	Location:	Weapon:	Sights:	Notes:

Date:	A Zone: Body / Head	# Under Par:	# In A Box:	Go / No Go
	Location:	Weapon:	Sights:	Notes:

Date:	A Zone: Body / Head	# Under Par:	# In A Box:	Go / No Go
	Location:	Weapon:	Sights:	Notes:

Date:	A Zone: Body / Head	# Under Par:	# In A Box:	Go / No Go
	Location:	Weapon:	Sights:	Notes:

Date:	A Zone: Body / Head	# Under Par:	# In A Box:	Go / No Go
	Location:	Weapon:	Sights:	Notes:

READY PISTOL

Date:	Location:	Weapon:	Sights:	Notes:
A Zone: Body / Head	# Under Par:	# In A Box:	**Go / No Go**	

Date:	Location:	Weapon:	Sights:	Notes:
A Zone: Body / Head	# Under Par:	# In A Box:	**Go / No Go**	

Date:	Location:	Weapon:	Sights:	Notes:
A Zone: Body / Head	# Under Par:	# In A Box:	**Go / No Go**	

Date:	Location:	Weapon:	Sights:	Notes:
A Zone: Body / Head	# Under Par:	# In A Box:	**Go / No Go**	

Date:	Location:	Weapon:	Sights:	Notes:
A Zone: Body / Head	# Under Par:	# In A Box:	**Go / No Go**	

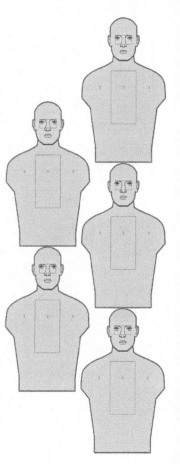

READY PISTOL

Date:	Location:	Weapon:	Sights:	Notes:
A Zone: Body / Head	# Under Par:	# In A Box:	Go / No Go	

Date:	Location:	Weapon:	Sights:	Notes:
A Zone: Body / Head	# Under Par:	# In A Box:	Go / No Go	

Date:	Location:	Weapon:	Sights:	Notes:
A Zone: Body / Head	# Under Par:	# In A Box:	Go / No Go	

Date:	Location:	Weapon:	Sights:	Notes:
A Zone: Body / Head	# Under Par:	# In A Box:	Go / No Go	

Date:	Location:	Weapon:	Sights:	Notes:
A Zone: Body / Head	# Under Par:	# In A Box:	Go / No Go	

READY PISTOL

Date:	Location:	Weapon:	Sights:	Notes:
A Zone: Body / Head	# Under Par:	# In A Box:	**Go / No Go**	

Date:	Location:	Weapon:	Sights:	Notes:
A Zone: Body / Head	# Under Par:	# In A Box:	**Go / No Go**	

Date:	Location:	Weapon:	Sights:	Notes:
A Zone: Body / Head	# Under Par:	# In A Box:	**Go / No Go**	

Date:	Location:	Weapon:	Sights:	Notes:
A Zone: Body / Head	# Under Par:	# In A Box:	**Go / No Go**	

Date:	Location:	Weapon:	Sights:	Notes:
A Zone: Body / Head	# Under Par:	# In A Box:	**Go / No Go**	

HIGH READY PISTOL

Purpose: To increase competency of the use of the high ready position.

Distance: 10 Yards.

Target: JD-QUAL1

Par Time: 1 Second.

Extra Equipment Needed: Shot timer.

Rounds Fired Per Rep: 1 Round.   **Total Rounds Fired:** 5 Rounds.

Point Penalty: Go / No Go.

Repetitions: 5 Reps.

Starting Position & Condition: Standing - High ready. Condition 1.

Description: The high ready position is where the pistols muzzle is pointed in the upward at a roughly 60 degrees angle at direction of the target while you are looking at the target just over the top of the front sight. From the high ready position, at the timer beep, raise the pistol and take aim at the target with a flash sight picture and fire a round within 1 second into the A Zone (5 point) body box. Record how many times you made par time and hit within the A Zone (5 point) body box.

Goals: Novice: All shots in body under par.   Expert: All shots in body A Zone under par.   Gunfighter: All shots in head A zone under par.

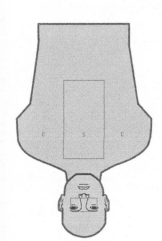

HIGH READY PISTOL

Date:	Location:	Weapon:	Sights:	Notes:
A Zone: Body / Head	# Under Par:	# In A Box:	**Go / No Go**	

Date:	Location:	Weapon:	Sights:	Notes:
A Zone: Body / Head	# Under Par:	# In A Box:	**Go / No Go**	

Date:	Location:	Weapon:	Sights:	Notes:
A Zone: Body / Head	# Under Par:	# In A Box:	**Go / No Go**	

Date:	Location:	Weapon:	Sights:	Notes:
A Zone: Body / Head	# Under Par:	# In A Box:	**Go / No Go**	

Date:	Location:	Weapon:	Sights:	Notes:
A Zone: Body / Head	# Under Par:	# In A Box:	**Go / No Go**	

HIGH READY PISTOL

Date:	Location:	Weapon:	Sights:	Notes:
A Zone: Body / Head	# Under Par:	# In A Box:	**Go / No Go**	

Date:	Location:	Weapon:	Sights:	Notes:
A Zone: Body / Head	# Under Par:	# In A Box:	**Go / No Go**	

Date:	Location:	Weapon:	Sights:	Notes:
A Zone: Body / Head	# Under Par:	# In A Box:	**Go / No Go**	

Date:	Location:	Weapon:	Sights:	Notes:
A Zone: Body / Head	# Under Par:	# In A Box:	**Go / No Go**	

Date:	Location:	Weapon:	Sights:	Notes:
A Zone: Body / Head	# Under Par:	# In A Box:	**Go / No Go**	

HIGH READY PISTOL

Date:	Location:	Weapon:	Sights:	Notes:
A Zone: Body / Head	# Under Par:	# In A Box:	**Go / No Go**	

Date:	Location:	Weapon:	Sights:	Notes:
A Zone: Body / Head	# Under Par:	# In A Box:	**Go / No Go**	

Date:	Location:	Weapon:	Sights:	Notes:
A Zone: Body / Head	# Under Par:	# In A Box:	**Go / No Go**	

Date:	Location:	Weapon:	Sights:	Notes:
A Zone: Body / Head	# Under Par:	# In A Box:	**Go / No Go**	

Date:	Location:	Weapon:	Sights:	Notes:
A Zone: Body / Head	# Under Par:	# In A Box:	**Go / No Go**	

HIGH READY PISTOL

A Zone: Body / Head	# Under Par:	# In A Box:	Go / No Go	
Date:	Location:	Weapon:	Sights:	Notes:

A Zone: Body / Head	# Under Par:	# In A Box:	Go / No Go	
Date:	Location:	Weapon:	Sights:	Notes:

A Zone: Body / Head	# Under Par:	# In A Box:	Go / No Go	
Date:	Location:	Weapon:	Sights:	Notes:

A Zone: Body / Head	# Under Par:	# In A Box:	Go / No Go	
Date:	Location:	Weapon:	Sights:	Notes:

A Zone: Body / Head	# Under Par:	# In A Box:	Go / No Go	
Date:	Location:	Weapon:	Sights:	Notes:

HIGH READY PISTOL

Date:	Location:	Weapon:	Sights:	Notes:
A Zone: Body / Head	# Under Par:	# In A Box:	**Go / No Go**	

Date:	Location:	Weapon:	Sights:	Notes:
A Zone: Body / Head	# Under Par:	# In A Box:	**Go / No Go**	

Date:	Location:	Weapon:	Sights:	Notes:
A Zone: Body / Head	# Under Par:	# In A Box:	**Go / No Go**	

Date:	Location:	Weapon:	Sights:	Notes:
A Zone: Body / Head	# Under Par:	# In A Box:	**Go / No Go**	

Date:	Location:	Weapon:	Sights:	Notes:
A Zone: Body / Head	# Under Par:	# In A Box:	**Go / No Go**	

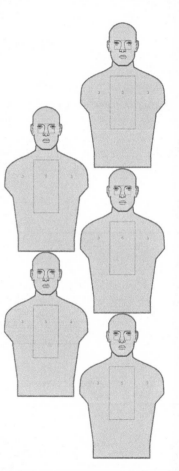

TACTICAL READY PISTOL

Purpose: To increase competency of the use of the tactical ready position.

Distance: 10 Yards.

Target: JD-QUAL1

Par Time: 1.2 Second.

Extra Equipment Needed: Shot timer.

Rounds Fired Per Rep: 1 Round.   **Total Rounds Fired:** 5 Rounds.

Point Penalty: Go / No Go.

Repetitions: 5 Reps.

Starting Position & Condition: Standing - Tactical ready. Condition 1.

Description: The tactical ready position is where the pistol is brought back to your chest, laid on it's side with the muzzle pointed in the direction of the ground 6 to 8 inches in front of your feet. Your support hand will be behind the pistol laid on your chest making a diamond shape with your thumbs touching and your fingers touching. From the tactical ready position, at the timer beep, raise the pistol and take aim at the target with a flash sight picture and fire a round within 1.2 second into the A Zone (5 point) body box. Record how many times you made par time and hit within the A Zone (5 point) body box.

Goals: Novice: All shots in body under par.   Expert: All shots in body A Zone under par.   Gunfighter: All shots in head A Zone under par.

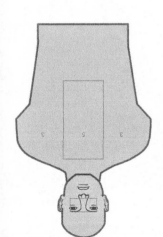

TACTICAL READY PISTOL

Date:	Location:	Weapon:	Sights:	Notes:
A Zone: Body / Head	# Under Par:	# In A Box:	**Go / No Go**	

Date:	Location:	Weapon:	Sights:	Notes:
A Zone: Body / Head	# Under Par:	# In A Box:	**Go / No Go**	

Date:	Location:	Weapon:	Sights:	Notes:
A Zone: Body / Head	# Under Par:	# In A Box:	**Go / No Go**	

Date:	Location:	Weapon:	Sights:	Notes:
A Zone: Body / Head	# Under Par:	# In A Box:	**Go / No Go**	

Date:	Location:	Weapon:	Sights:	Notes:
A Zone: Body / Head	# Under Par:	# In A Box:	**Go / No Go**	

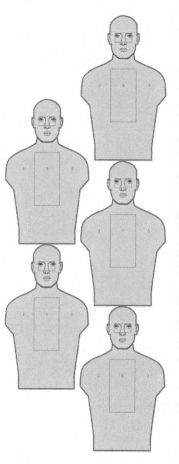

TACTICAL READY PISTOL

Date:	Location:	Weapon:	Sights:	Notes:
A Zone: Body / Head	# Under Par:	# In A Box:	**Go / No Go**	

Date:	Location:	Weapon:	Sights:	Notes:
A Zone: Body / Head	# Under Par:	# In A Box:	**Go / No Go**	

Date:	Location:	Weapon:	Sights:	Notes:
A Zone: Body / Head	# Under Par:	# In A Box:	**Go / No Go**	

Date:	Location:	Weapon:	Sights:	Notes:
A Zone: Body / Head	# Under Par:	# In A Box:	**Go / No Go**	

Date:	Location:	Weapon:	Sights:	Notes:
A Zone: Body / Head	# Under Par:	# In A Box:	**Go / No Go**	

TACTICAL READY PISTOL

Date:	Location:	Weapon:	Sights:	Notes:
A Zone: Body / Head	# Under Par:	# In A Box:	**Go / No Go**	

Date:	Location:	Weapon:	Sights:	Notes:
A Zone: Body / Head	# Under Par:	# In A Box:	**Go / No Go**	

Date:	Location:	Weapon:	Sights:	Notes:
A Zone: Body / Head	# Under Par:	# In A Box:	**Go / No Go**	

Date:	Location:	Weapon:	Sights:	Notes:
A Zone: Body / Head	# Under Par:	# In A Box:	**Go / No Go**	

Date:	Location:	Weapon:	Sights:	Notes:
A Zone: Body / Head	# Under Par:	# In A Box:	**Go / No Go**	

A Zone: Body / Head	# Under Par:	# In A Box:	Go / No Go
Date:	Location:	Weapon:	Sights:	Notes:

A Zone: Body / Head	# Under Par:	# In A Box:	Go / No Go
Date:	Location:	Weapon:	Sights:	Notes:

A Zone: Body / Head	# Under Par:	# In A Box:	Go / No Go
Date:	Location:	Weapon:	Sights:	Notes:

A Zone: Body / Head	# Under Par:	# In A Box:	Go / No Go
Date:	Location:	Weapon:	Sights:	Notes:

A Zone: Body / Head	# Under Par:	# In A Box:	Go / No Go
Date:	Location:	Weapon:	Sights:	Notes:

TACTICAL READY PISTOL

Date:	Location:	Weapon:	Sights:	Notes:
A Zone: Body / Head	# Under Par:	# In A Box:	**Go / No Go**	

Date:	Location:	Weapon:	Sights:	Notes:
A Zone: Body / Head	# Under Par:	# In A Box:	**Go / No Go**	

Date:	Location:	Weapon:	Sights:	Notes:
A Zone: Body / Head	# Under Par:	# In A Box:	**Go / No Go**	

Date:	Location:	Weapon:	Sights:	Notes:
A Zone: Body / Head	# Under Par:	# In A Box:	**Go / No Go**	

Date:	Location:	Weapon:	Sights:	Notes:
A Zone: Body / Head	# Under Par:	# In A Box:	**Go / No Go**	

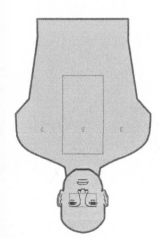

KNEEL

Purpose: To increase competency of the use of the kneeling position.

Distance: 25 Yards.

Target: JD-QUAL1

Par Time: 5 Seconds.

Extra Equipment Needed: Shot timer.

Rounds Fired Per Rep: 3 Rounds.   **Total Rounds Fired:** 15 Rounds.

Point Penalty: Go / No Go.

Repetitions: 5 Reps.

Starting Position & Condition: Standing to kneeling. Condition 1.

Description: From the standing position, at the timer beep, draw and go to the kneeling position while keeping the pistol pointed down range at the targets direction. Take aim at the target and fire 3 rounds into the A Zone (5 point) body box. Record how many times you made par time and hit within the A Zone (5 point) body box.

Goals: Novice: All shots in body under par.   Expert: All shots in body A Zone under par.   Gunfighter: All shots in head A zone under par.

KNEEL

Date:	Location:	Weapon:	Sights:	A Box: Head / Body
Rep 1 Time:	Rep 2 Time:	Rep 3 Time:	Rep 4 Time:	Rep 5 Time:
Shots under par:	Shots under par:	Shots under par:	Shots under par:	Shots under par:
Rep 1 Score:	Rep 2 Score:	Rep 3 Score:	Rep 4 Score:	Rep 5 Score:
Total # of shots under par:		**Total Score:**		Notes:

Date:	Location:	Weapon:	Sights:	A Box: Head / Body
Rep 1 Time:	Rep 2 Time:	Rep 3 Time:	Rep 4 Time:	Rep 5 Time:
Shots under par:	Shots under par:	Shots under par:	Shots under par:	Shots under par:
Rep 1 Score:	Rep 2 Score:	Rep 3 Score:	Rep 4 Score:	Rep 5 Score:
Total # of shots under par:		**Total Score:**		Notes:

Date:	Location:	Weapon:	Sights:	A Box: Head / Body
Rep 1 Time:	Rep 2 Time:	Rep 3 Time:	Rep 4 Time:	Rep 5 Time:
Shots under par:	Shots under par:	Shots under par:	Shots under par:	Shots under par:
Rep 1 Score:	Rep 2 Score:	Rep 3 Score:	Rep 4 Score:	Rep 5 Score:
Total # of shots under par:		**Total Score:**		Notes:

KNEEL

Date:	Location:	Weapon:	Sights:	A Box: Head / Body
Rep 1 Time:	Rep 2 Time:	Rep 3 Time:	Rep 4 Time:	Rep 5 Time:
Shots under par:	Shots under par:	Shots under par:	Shots under par:	Shots under par:
Rep 1 Score:	Rep 2 Score:	Rep 3 Score:	Rep 4 Score:	Rep 5 Score:
Total # of shots under par:		Total Score:		Notes:

Date:	Location:	Weapon:	Sights:	A Box: Head / Body
Rep 1 Time:	Rep 2 Time:	Rep 3 Time:	Rep 4 Time:	Rep 5 Time:
Shots under par:	Shots under par:	Shots under par:	Shots under par:	Shots under par:
Rep 1 Score:	Rep 2 Score:	Rep 3 Score:	Rep 4 Score:	Rep 5 Score:
Total # of shots under par:		Total Score:		Notes:

Date:	Location:	Weapon:	Sights:	A Box: Head / Body
Rep 1 Time:	Rep 2 Time:	Rep 3 Time:	Rep 4 Time:	Rep 5 Time:
Shots under par:	Shots under par:	Shots under par:	Shots under par:	Shots under par:
Rep 1 Score:	Rep 2 Score:	Rep 3 Score:	Rep 4 Score:	Rep 5 Score:
Total # of shots under par:		Total Score:		Notes:

KNEEL

Date:	Location:	Weapon:	Sights:	A Box: Head / Body
Rep 1 Time:	Rep 2 Time:	Rep 3 Time:	Rep 4 Time:	Rep 5 Time:
Shots under par:	Shots under par:	Shots under par:	Shots under par:	Shots under par:
Rep 1 Score:	Rep 2 Score:	Rep 3 Score:	Rep 4 Score:	Rep 5 Score:
Total # of shots under par:		**Total Score:**		Notes:

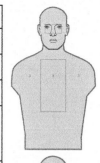

Date:	Location:	Weapon:	Sights:	A Box: Head / Body
Rep 1 Time:	Rep 2 Time:	Rep 3 Time:	Rep 4 Time:	Rep 5 Time:
Shots under par:	Shots under par:	Shots under par:	Shots under par:	Shots under par:
Rep 1 Score:	Rep 2 Score:	Rep 3 Score:	Rep 4 Score:	Rep 5 Score:
Total # of shots under par:		**Total Score:**		Notes:

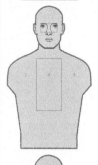

Date:	Location:	Weapon:	Sights:	A Box: Head / Body
Rep 1 Time:	Rep 2 Time:	Rep 3 Time:	Rep 4 Time:	Rep 5 Time:
Shots under par:	Shots under par:	Shots under par:	Shots under par:	Shots under par:
Rep 1 Score:	Rep 2 Score:	Rep 3 Score:	Rep 4 Score:	Rep 5 Score:
Total # of shots under par:		**Total Score:**		Notes:

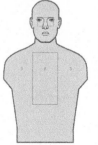

KNEEL

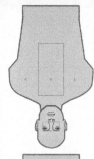

Date:	Location:	Weapon:	Sights:	A Box: Head / Body
Rep 1 Time:	Rep 2 Time:	Rep 3 Time:	Rep 4 Time:	Rep 5 Time:
Shots under par:	Shots under par:	Shots under par:	Shots under par:	Shots under par:
Rep 1 Score:	Rep 2 Score:	Rep 3 Score:	Rep 4 Score:	Rep 5 Score:
Total # of shots under par:		**Total Score:**		Notes:

Date:	Location:	Weapon:	Sights:	A Box: Head / Body
Rep 1 Time:	Rep 2 Time:	Rep 3 Time:	Rep 4 Time:	Rep 5 Time:
Shots under par:	Shots under par:	Shots under par:	Shots under par:	Shots under par:
Rep 1 Score:	Rep 2 Score:	Rep 3 Score:	Rep 4 Score:	Rep 5 Score:
Total # of shots under par:		**Total Score:**		Notes:

Date:	Location:	Weapon:	Sights:	A Box: Head / Body
Rep 1 Time:	Rep 2 Time:	Rep 3 Time:	Rep 4 Time:	Rep 5 Time:
Shots under par:	Shots under par:	Shots under par:	Shots under par:	Shots under par:
Rep 1 Score:	Rep 2 Score:	Rep 3 Score:	Rep 4 Score:	Rep 5 Score:
Total # of shots under par:		**Total Score:**		Notes:

KNEEL

Date:	Location:	Weapon:	Sights:	A Box: Head / Body
Rep 1 Time:	Rep 2 Time:	Rep 3 Time:	Rep 4 Time:	Rep 5 Time:
Shots under par:	Shots under par:	Shots under par:	Shots under par:	Shots under par:
Rep 1 Score:	Rep 2 Score:	Rep 3 Score:	Rep 4 Score:	Rep 5 Score:
Total # of shots under par:		**Total Score:**		Notes:

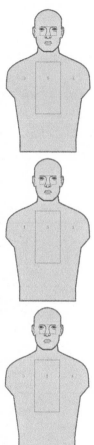

Date:	Location:	Weapon:	Sights:	A Box: Head / Body
Rep 1 Time:	Rep 2 Time:	Rep 3 Time:	Rep 4 Time:	Rep 5 Time:
Shots under par:	Shots under par:	Shots under par:	Shots under par:	Shots under par:
Rep 1 Score:	Rep 2 Score:	Rep 3 Score:	Rep 4 Score:	Rep 5 Score:
Total # of shots under par:		**Total Score:**		Notes:

Date:	Location:	Weapon:	Sights:	A Box: Head / Body
Rep 1 Time:	Rep 2 Time:	Rep 3 Time:	Rep 4 Time:	Rep 5 Time:
Shots under par:	Shots under par:	Shots under par:	Shots under par:	Shots under par:
Rep 1 Score:	Rep 2 Score:	Rep 3 Score:	Rep 4 Score:	Rep 5 Score:
Total # of shots under par:		**Total Score:**		Notes:

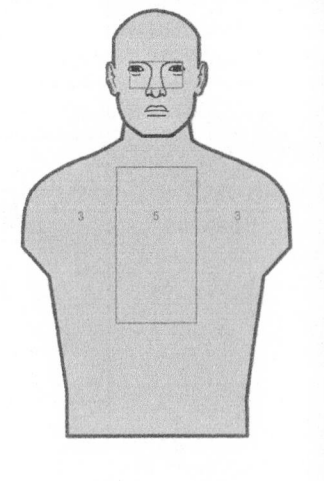

THE SQUAT

Purpose: To increase competency of the use of the squatting position.

Distance: 25 Yards.

Target: JD-QUAL1

Par Time: 5 Seconds.

Extra Equipment Needed: Shot timer.

Rounds Fired Per Rep: 3 Rounds.   **Total Rounds Fired:** 15 Rounds.

Point Penalty: Go / No Go.

Repetitions: 5 Reps.

Starting Position & Condition: Standing to squatting. Condition 1.

Description: From the standing position, at the timer beep, draw and go to a squatting position while keeping the pistol pointed down range at the targets direction. Take aim at the target and fire 3 rounds into the A Zone (5 point) body box. Record how many times you made par time and hit within the A Zone (5 point) body box.

Goals: Novice: All shots in body under par.   Expert: All shots in body A Zone under par.   Gunfighter: All shots in head A zone under par.

THE SQUAT

Date:	Location:	Weapon:	Sights:	A Box: Head / Body
Rep 1 Time:	Rep 2 Time:	Rep 3 Time:	Rep 4 Time:	Rep 5 Time:
Shots under par:	Shots under par:	Shots under par:	Shots under par:	Shots under par:
Rep 1 Score:	Rep 2 Score:	Rep 3 Score:	Rep 4 Score:	Rep 5 Score:
Total # of shots under par:		**Total Score:**		Notes:

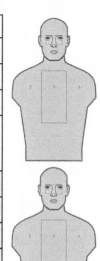

Date:	Location:	Weapon:	Sights:	A Box: Head / Body
Rep 1 Time:	Rep 2 Time:	Rep 3 Time:	Rep 4 Time:	Rep 5 Time:
Shots under par:	Shots under par:	Shots under par:	Shots under par:	Shots under par:
Rep 1 Score:	Rep 2 Score:	Rep 3 Score:	Rep 4 Score:	Rep 5 Score:
Total # of shots under par:		**Total Score:**		Notes:

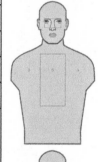

Date:	Location:	Weapon:	Sights:	A Box: Head / Body
Rep 1 Time:	Rep 2 Time:	Rep 3 Time:	Rep 4 Time:	Rep 5 Time:
Shots under par:	Shots under par:	Shots under par:	Shots under par:	Shots under par:
Rep 1 Score:	Rep 2 Score:	Rep 3 Score:	Rep 4 Score:	Rep 5 Score:
Total # of shots under par:		**Total Score:**		Notes:

THE SQUAT

Date:	Location:	Weapon:	Sights:	A Box: Head / Body
Rep 1 Time:	Rep 2 Time:	Rep 3 Time:	Rep 4 Time:	Rep 5 Time:
Shots under par:	Shots under par:	Shots under par:	Shots under par:	Shots under par:
Rep 1 Score:	Rep 2 Score:	Rep 3 Score:	Rep 4 Score:	Rep 5 Score:
Total # of shots under par:	Total Score:		Notes:	

Date:	Location:	Weapon:	Sights:	A Box: Head / Body
Rep 1 Time:	Rep 2 Time:	Rep 3 Time:	Rep 4 Time:	Rep 5 Time:
Shots under par:	Shots under par:	Shots under par:	Shots under par:	Shots under par:
Rep 1 Score:	Rep 2 Score:	Rep 3 Score:	Rep 4 Score:	Rep 5 Score:
Total # of shots under par:	Total Score:		Notes:	

Date:	Location:	Weapon:	Sights:	A Box: Head / Body
Rep 1 Time:	Rep 2 Time:	Rep 3 Time:	Rep 4 Time:	Rep 5 Time:
Shots under par:	Shots under par:	Shots under par:	Shots under par:	Shots under par:
Rep 1 Score:	Rep 2 Score:	Rep 3 Score:	Rep 4 Score:	Rep 5 Score:
Total # of shots under par:	Total Score:		Notes:	

THE SQUAT

Date:	Location:	Weapon:	Sights:	A Box: Head / Body
Rep 1 Time:	Rep 2 Time:	Rep 3 Time:	Rep 4 Time:	Rep 5 Time:
Shots under par:	Shots under par:	Shots under par:	Shots under par:	Shots under par:
Rep 1 Score:	Rep 2 Score:	Rep 3 Score:	Rep 4 Score:	Rep 5 Score:
Total # of shots under par:		**Total Score:**		Notes:

Date:	Location:	Weapon:	Sights:	A Box: Head / Body
Rep 1 Time:	Rep 2 Time:	Rep 3 Time:	Rep 4 Time:	Rep 5 Time:
Shots under par:	Shots under par:	Shots under par:	Shots under par:	Shots under par:
Rep 1 Score:	Rep 2 Score:	Rep 3 Score:	Rep 4 Score:	Rep 5 Score:
Total # of shots under par:		**Total Score:**		Notes:

Date:	Location:	Weapon:	Sights:	A Box: Head / Body
Rep 1 Time:	Rep 2 Time:	Rep 3 Time:	Rep 4 Time:	Rep 5 Time:
Shots under par:	Shots under par:	Shots under par:	Shots under par:	Shots under par:
Rep 1 Score:	Rep 2 Score:	Rep 3 Score:	Rep 4 Score:	Rep 5 Score:
Total # of shots under par:		**Total Score:**		Notes:

THE SQUAT

Date:	Location:	Weapon:	Sights:	A Box: Head / Body
Rep 1 Time:	Rep 2 Time:	Rep 3 Time:	Rep 4 Time:	Rep 5 Time:
Shots under par:	Shots under par:	Shots under par:	Shots under par:	Shots under par:
Rep 1 Score:	Rep 2 Score:	Rep 3 Score:	Rep 4 Score:	Rep 5 Score:
Total # of shots under par:		Total Score:		Notes:

Date:	Location:	Weapon:	Sights:	A Box: Head / Body
Rep 1 Time:	Rep 2 Time:	Rep 3 Time:	Rep 4 Time:	Rep 5 Time:
Shots under par:	Shots under par:	Shots under par:	Shots under par:	Shots under par:
Rep 1 Score:	Rep 2 Score:	Rep 3 Score:	Rep 4 Score:	Rep 5 Score:
Total # of shots under par:		Total Score:		Notes:

Date:	Location:	Weapon:	Sights:	A Box: Head / Body
Rep 1 Time:	Rep 2 Time:	Rep 3 Time:	Rep 4 Time:	Rep 5 Time:
Shots under par:	Shots under par:	Shots under par:	Shots under par:	Shots under par:
Rep 1 Score:	Rep 2 Score:	Rep 3 Score:	Rep 4 Score:	Rep 5 Score:
Total # of shots under par:		Total Score:		Notes:

THE SQUAT

Date:	Location:	Weapon:	Sights:	A Box: Head / Body
Rep 1 Time:	Rep 2 Time:	Rep 3 Time:	Rep 4 Time:	Rep 5 Time:
Shots under par:	Shots under par:	Shots under par:	Shots under par:	Shots under par:
Rep 1 Score:	Rep 2 Score:	Rep 3 Score:	Rep 4 Score:	Rep 5 Score:
Total # of shots under par:		**Total Score:**		Notes:

Date:	Location:	Weapon:	Sights:	A Box: Head / Body
Rep 1 Time:	Rep 2 Time:	Rep 3 Time:	Rep 4 Time:	Rep 5 Time:
Shots under par:	Shots under par:	Shots under par:	Shots under par:	Shots under par:
Rep 1 Score:	Rep 2 Score:	Rep 3 Score:	Rep 4 Score:	Rep 5 Score:
Total # of shots under par:		**Total Score:**		Notes:

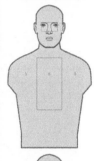

Date:	Location:	Weapon:	Sights:	A Box: Head / Body
Rep 1 Time:	Rep 2 Time:	Rep 3 Time:	Rep 4 Time:	Rep 5 Time:
Shots under par:	Shots under par:	Shots under par:	Shots under par:	Shots under par:
Rep 1 Score:	Rep 2 Score:	Rep 3 Score:	Rep 4 Score:	Rep 5 Score:
Total # of shots under par:		**Total Score:**		Notes:

CADENCE

Purpose: Increase consistent shot cadence and shot speed.

Distance: 7 Yards.

Target: JD-QUAL1

Total Rounds Fired: 45 Rounds.

Point penalty: As per target.

Starting Position & Condition: Standing - Low ready. Condition 1.

Description: Aim and fire the described number of rounds into the (5 point) A Zone body box. After you are done firing all of the 4 stages, record your score. For highly advanced shooters, put your rounds in the (5 point) A Zone head box. Goal is all hits in (5 point) A Zone body box and make par time.

- Stage 1 – Fire 1 round in a 1 second par time X 5 repetitions.

- Stage 2 – Fire 2 rounds in a 1.3 second par time X 5 repetitions.

- Stage 3 – Fire 3 rounds in a 1.6 second par time X 5 repetitions.

- Stage 4 – Fire 5 rounds in a 2.5 second par time X 3 repetitions.

Goals: Novice: All shots in body.   **Expert:** All shots in body A box.   **Gunfighter:** All shots in head A box.

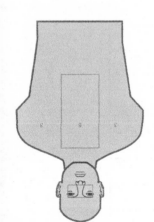

CADENCE

Date:	Location:	Weapon:	Sights:	A Box: Head / Body
Stage 1 Score:	Stage 2 Score:	Stage 3 Score:	Stage 4 Score:	**Total Score:**
Shots over par:	Shots over par:	Shots over par:	Shots over par:	Notes:
# Outside A box:	# Outside A box:	# Outside A box:	# Outside A box:	

Date:	Location:	Weapon:	Sights:	A Box: Head / Body
Stage 1 Score:	Stage 2 Score:	Stage 3 Score:	Stage 4 Score:	**Total Score:**
Shots over par:	Shots over par:	Shots over par:	Shots over par:	Notes:
# Outside A box:	# Outside A box:	# Outside A box:	# Outside A box:	

Date:	Location:	Weapon:	Sights:	A Box: Head / Body
Stage 1 Score:	Stage 2 Score:	Stage 3 Score:	Stage 4 Score:	**Total Score:**
Shots over par:	Shots over par:	Shots over par:	Shots over par:	Notes:
# Outside A box:	# Outside A box:	# Outside A box:	# Outside A box:	

CADENCE

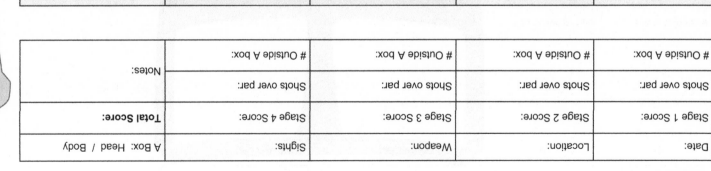

Date:	Location:	Weapon:	Sights:	A Box: Head / Body
Stage 1 Score:	Stage 2 Score:	Stage 3 Score:	Stage 4 Score:	Total Score:
Shots over par:	Shots over par:	Shots over par:	Shots over par:	Notes:
# Outside A box:	# Outside A box:	# Outside A box:	# Outside A box:	

Date:	Location:	Weapon:	Sights:	A Box: Head / Body
Stage 1 Score:	Stage 2 Score:	Stage 3 Score:	Stage 4 Score:	Total Score:
Shots over par:	Shots over par:	Shots over par:	Shots over par:	Notes:
# Outside A box:	# Outside A box:	# Outside A box:	# Outside A box:	

Date:	Location:	Weapon:	Sights:	A Box: Head / Body
Stage 1 Score:	Stage 2 Score:	Stage 3 Score:	Stage 4 Score:	Total Score:
Shots over par:	Shots over par:	Shots over par:	Shots over par:	Notes:
# Outside A box:	# Outside A box:	# Outside A box:	# Outside A box:	

CADENCE

Date:	Location:	Weapon:	Sights:	A Box: Head / Body
Stage 1 Score:	Stage 2 Score:	Stage 3 Score:	Stage 4 Score:	**Total Score:**
Shots over par:	Shots over par:	Shots over par:	Shots over par:	Notes:
# Outside A box:	# Outside A box:	# Outside A box:	# Outside A box:	

Date:	Location:	Weapon:	Sights:	A Box: Head / Body
Stage 1 Score:	Stage 2 Score:	Stage 3 Score:	Stage 4 Score:	**Total Score:**
Shots over par:	Shots over par:	Shots over par:	Shots over par:	Notes:
# Outside A box:	# Outside A box:	# Outside A box:	# Outside A box:	

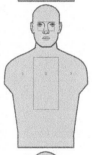

Date:	Location:	Weapon:	Sights:	A Box: Head / Body
Stage 1 Score:	Stage 2 Score:	Stage 3 Score:	Stage 4 Score:	**Total Score:**
Shots over par:	Shots over par:	Shots over par:	Shots over par:	Notes:
# Outside A box:	# Outside A box:	# Outside A box:	# Outside A box:	

CADENCE

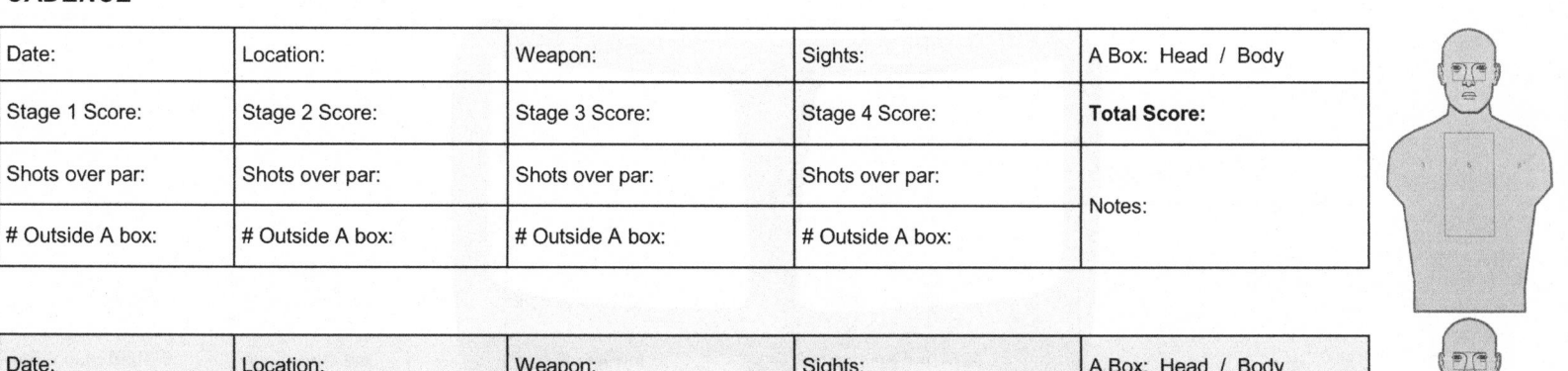

Date:	Location:	Weapon:	Sights:	A Box: Head / Body
Stage 1 Score:	Stage 2 Score:	Stage 3 Score:	Stage 4 Score:	**Total Score:**
Shots over par:	Shots over par:	Shots over par:	Shots over par:	Notes:
# Outside A box:	# Outside A box:	# Outside A box:	# Outside A box:	

Date:	Location:	Weapon:	Sights:	A Box: Head / Body
Stage 1 Score:	Stage 2 Score:	Stage 3 Score:	Stage 4 Score:	**Total Score:**
Shots over par:	Shots over par:	Shots over par:	Shots over par:	Notes:
# Outside A box:	# Outside A box:	# Outside A box:	# Outside A box:	

Date:	Location:	Weapon:	Sights:	A Box: Head / Body
Stage 1 Score:	Stage 2 Score:	Stage 3 Score:	Stage 4 Score:	**Total Score:**
Shots over par:	Shots over par:	Shots over par:	Shots over par:	Notes:
# Outside A box:	# Outside A box:	# Outside A box:	# Outside A box:	

CADENCE

Date:	Location:	Weapon:	Sights:	A Box: Head / Body
Stage 1 Score:	Stage 2 Score:	Stage 3 Score:	Stage 4 Score:	**Total Score:**
Shots over par:	Shots over par:	Shots over par:	Shots over par:	Notes:
# Outside A box:	# Outside A box:	# Outside A box:	# Outside A box:	

Date:	Location:	Weapon:	Sights:	A Box: Head / Body
Stage 1 Score:	Stage 2 Score:	Stage 3 Score:	Stage 4 Score:	**Total Score:**
Shots over par:	Shots over par:	Shots over par:	Shots over par:	Notes:
# Outside A box:	# Outside A box:	# Outside A box:	# Outside A box:	

Date:	Location:	Weapon:	Sights:	A Box: Head / Body
Stage 1 Score:	Stage 2 Score:	Stage 3 Score:	Stage 4 Score:	**Total Score:**
Shots over par:	Shots over par:	Shots over par:	Shots over par:	Notes:
# Outside A box:	# Outside A box:	# Outside A box:	# Outside A box:	

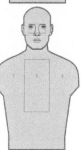

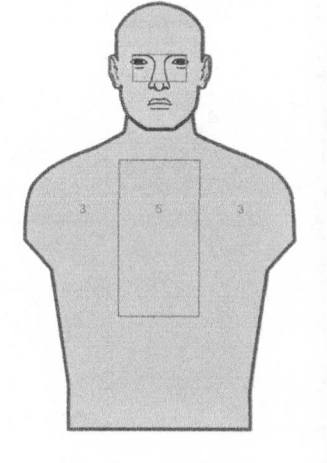

HAVE A NICE DAY

Purpose: Increase accuracy and recoil management.

Distance: 15 Yards.

Target: JD-QUAL1

Par Time: 15 Seconds.

Extra Equipment Needed: Shot timer.

Total Rounds Fired: 15 Rounds.

Point Penalty: As per target score.

Repetitions: 1 Rep.

Starting Position & Condition: Standing - Low ready. Condition 1.

Description: At the timer beep, fire 10 rounds into the A Zone (5 point) body box and 5 rounds into the A Zone (5 point) head box.

Goals: Novice: 60 points under par.   Expert: 69 points under par.   Gunfighter: 75 points under 10 seconds.

HAVE A NICE DAY

Date:	Location:	Weapon:	Sights:	Notes:
Under par: Y / N	All A Zone: Y / N	Time:	**Total Score:**	

Date:	Location:	Weapon:	Sights:	Notes:
Under par: Y / N	All A Zone: Y / N	Time:	**Total Score:**	

Date:	Location:	Weapon:	Sights:	Notes:
Under par: Y / N	All A Zone: Y / N	Time:	**Total Score:**	

Date:	Location:	Weapon:	Sights:	Notes:
Under par: Y / N	All A Zone: Y / N	Time:	**Total Score:**	

Date:	Location:	Weapon:	Sights:	Notes:
Under par: Y / N	All A Zone: Y / N	Time:	**Total Score:**	

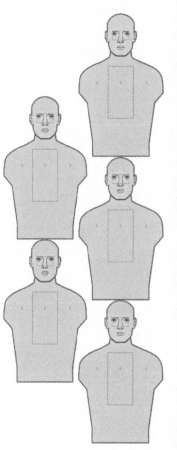

HAVE A NICE DAY

Date:	Location:	Weapon:	Sights:	Notes:
Under par: Y / N	All A Zone: Y / N	Time:	**Total Score:**	

Date:	Location:	Weapon:	Sights:	Notes:
Under par: Y / N	All A Zone: Y / N	Time:	**Total Score:**	

Date:	Location:	Weapon:	Sights:	Notes:
Under par: Y / N	All A Zone: Y / N	Time:	**Total Score:**	

Date:	Location:	Weapon:	Sights:	Notes:
Under par: Y / N	All A Zone: Y / N	Time:	**Total Score:**	

Date:	Location:	Weapon:	Sights:	Notes:
Under par: Y / N	All A Zone: Y / N	Time:	**Total Score:**	

HAVE A NICE DAY

Date:	Location:	Weapon:	Sights:	Notes:
Under par: Y / N	All A Zone: Y / N	Time:	**Total Score:**	

Date:	Location:	Weapon:	Sights:	Notes:
Under par: Y / N	All A Zone: Y / N	Time:	**Total Score:**	

Date:	Location:	Weapon:	Sights:	Notes:
Under par: Y / N	All A Zone: Y / N	Time:	**Total Score:**	

Date:	Location:	Weapon:	Sights:	Notes:
Under par: Y / N	All A Zone: Y / N	Time:	**Total Score:**	

Date:	Location:	Weapon:	Sights:	Notes:
Under par: Y / N	All A Zone: Y / N	Time:	**Total Score:**	

HAVE A NICE DAY

Date:	Location:	Weapon:	Sights:	Notes:
Under par: Y / N	All A Zone: Y / N	Time:	**Total Score:**	

Date:	Location:	Weapon:	Sights:	Notes:
Under par: Y / N	All A Zone: Y / N	Time:	**Total Score:**	

Date:	Location:	Weapon:	Sights:	Notes:
Under par: Y / N	All A Zone: Y / N	Time:	**Total Score:**	

Date:	Location:	Weapon:	Sights:	Notes:
Under par: Y / N	All A Zone: Y / N	Time:	**Total Score:**	

Date:	Location:	Weapon:	Sights:	Notes:
Under par: Y / N	All A Zone: Y / N	Time:	**Total Score:**	

HAVE A NICE DAY

Date:	Location:	Weapon:	Sights:	Notes:
Under par: Y / N	All A Zone: Y / N	Time:	**Total Score:**	

Date:	Location:	Weapon:	Sights:	Notes:
Under par: Y / N	All A Zone: Y / N	Time:	**Total Score:**	

Date:	Location:	Weapon:	Sights:	Notes:
Under par: Y / N	All A Zone: Y / N	Time:	**Total Score:**	

Date:	Location:	Weapon:	Sights:	Notes:
Under par: Y / N	All A Zone: Y / N	Time:	**Total Score:**	

Date:	Location:	Weapon:	Sights:	Notes:
Under par: Y / N	All A Zone: Y / N	Time:	**Total Score:**	

HAMMER TIME

Purpose: Develop shot cadence.

Distance: 7 Yards.

Target: GF-1

Par Time: 3.5 Seconds.

Extra Equipment Needed: Shot timer.

Rounds Fired Per Rep: 5 Rounds.   **Total Rounds Fired:** 20 rounds.

Point Penalty: As per target score.

Repetitions: 4 Reps.

Starting Position & Condition: Standing - Low ready. Condition 1.

Description: At the timer beep, fire 5 rounds into the GF-1 target within 3.5 seconds.

Goals: Novice: 160 points under par.   Expert: 180 points under par.   Gunfighter: 200 points with 10 X's under par.

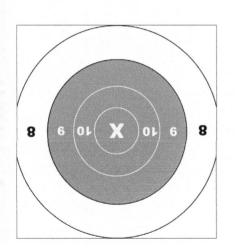

HAMMER TIME

Date:	Location:	Weapon:	Sites:	Ammo:	
Under Par: Y / N	Under Par: Y / N	Under Par: Y / N	Under Par: Y / N	Notes:	
Rep 1 Time:	Rep 2 Time:	Rep 3 Time:	Rep 4 Time:		
Rep 1 Score:	Rep 2 Score:	Rep 3 Score:	Rep 4 Score:	**Total Score:**	
Date:	Location:	Weapon:	Sites:	Ammo:	
Under Par: Y / N	Under Par: Y / N	Under Par: Y / N	Under Par: Y / N	Notes:	
Rep 1 Time:	Rep 2 Time:	Rep 3 Time:	Rep 4 Time:		
Rep 1 Score:	Rep 2 Score:	Rep 3 Score:	Rep 4 Score:	**Total Score:**	
Date:	Location:	Weapon:	Sites:	Ammo:	
Under Par: Y / N	Under Par: Y / N	Under Par: Y / N	Under Par: Y / N	Notes:	
Rep 1 Time:	Rep 2 Time:	Rep 3 Time:	Rep 4 Time:		
Rep 1 Score:	Rep 2 Score:	Rep 3 Score:	Rep 4 Score:	**Total Score:**	
Date:	Location:	Weapon:	Sites:	Ammo:	
Under Par: Y / N	Under Par: Y / N	Under Par: Y / N	Under Par: Y / N	Notes:	
Rep 1 Time:	Rep 2 Time:	Rep 3 Time:	Rep 4 Time:		
Rep 1 Score:	Rep 2 Score:	Rep 3 Score:	Rep 4 Score:	**Total Score:**	

HAMMER TIME

Date:	Location:	Weapon:	Sites:	Ammo:	
Under Par: Y / N	Under Par: Y / N	Under Par: Y / N	Under Par: Y / N	Notes:	
Rep 1 Time:	Rep 2 Time:	Rep 3 Time:	Rep 4 Time:		
Rep 1 Score:	Rep 2 Score:	Rep 3 Score:	Rep 4 Score:	**Total Score:**	
Date:	Location:	Weapon:	Sites:	Ammo:	
Under Par: Y / N	Under Par: Y / N	Under Par: Y / N	Under Par: Y / N	Notes:	
Rep 1 Time:	Rep 2 Time:	Rep 3 Time:	Rep 4 Time:		
Rep 1 Score:	Rep 2 Score:	Rep 3 Score:	Rep 4 Score:	**Total Score:**	
Date:	Location:	Weapon:	Sites:	Ammo:	
Under Par: Y / N	Under Par: Y / N	Under Par: Y / N	Under Par: Y / N	Notes:	
Rep 1 Time:	Rep 2 Time:	Rep 3 Time:	Rep 4 Time:		
Rep 1 Score:	Rep 2 Score:	Rep 3 Score:	Rep 4 Score:	**Total Score:**	
Date:	Location:	Weapon:	Sites:	Ammo:	
Under Par: Y / N	Under Par: Y / N	Under Par: Y / N	Under Par: Y / N	Notes:	
Rep 1 Time:	Rep 2 Time:	Rep 3 Time:	Rep 4 Time:		
Rep 1 Score:	Rep 2 Score:	Rep 3 Score:	Rep 4 Score:	**Total Score:**	

HAMMER TIME

Date:	Location:	Weapon:	Sites:	Ammo:	
Under Par: Y / N	Under Par: Y / N	Under Par: Y / N	Under Par: Y / N	Notes:	
Rep 1 Time:	Rep 2 Time:	Rep 3 Time:	Rep 4 Time:		
Rep 1 Score:	Rep 2 Score:	Rep 3 Score:	Rep 4 Score:	**Total Score:**	
Date:	Location:	Weapon:	Sites:	Ammo:	
Under Par: Y / N	Under Par: Y / N	Under Par: Y / N	Under Par: Y / N	Notes:	
Rep 1 Time:	Rep 2 Time:	Rep 3 Time:	Rep 4 Time:		
Rep 1 Score:	Rep 2 Score:	Rep 3 Score:	Rep 4 Score:	**Total Score:**	
Date:	Location:	Weapon:	Sites:	Ammo:	
Under Par: Y / N	Under Par: Y / N	Under Par: Y / N	Under Par: Y / N	Notes:	
Rep 1 Time:	Rep 2 Time:	Rep 3 Time:	Rep 4 Time:		
Rep 1 Score:	Rep 2 Score:	Rep 3 Score:	Rep 4 Score:	**Total Score:**	
Date:	Location:	Weapon:	Sites:	Ammo:	
Under Par: Y / N	Under Par: Y / N	Under Par: Y / N	Under Par: Y / N	Notes:	
Rep 1 Time:	Rep 2 Time:	Rep 3 Time:	Rep 4 Time:		
Rep 1 Score:	Rep 2 Score:	Rep 3 Score:	Rep 4 Score:	**Total Score:**	

Block 1

Date:	Location:	Weapon:	Sites:	Ammo:
Under Par: Y / N	Under Par: Y / N	Under Par: Y / N	Under Par: Y / N	Notes:
Rep 1 Time:	Rep 2 Time:	Rep 3 Time:	Rep 4 Time:	
Rep 1 Score:	Rep 2 Score:	Rep 3 Score:	Rep 4 Score:	**Total Score:**

Block 2

Date:	Location:	Weapon:	Sites:	Ammo:
Under Par: Y / N	Under Par: Y / N	Under Par: Y / N	Under Par: Y / N	Notes:
Rep 1 Time:	Rep 2 Time:	Rep 3 Time:	Rep 4 Time:	
Rep 1 Score:	Rep 2 Score:	Rep 3 Score:	Rep 4 Score:	**Total Score:**

Block 3

Date:	Location:	Weapon:	Sites:	Ammo:
Under Par: Y / N	Under Par: Y / N	Under Par: Y / N	Under Par: Y / N	Notes:
Rep 1 Time:	Rep 2 Time:	Rep 3 Time:	Rep 4 Time:	
Rep 1 Score:	Rep 2 Score:	Rep 3 Score:	Rep 4 Score:	**Total Score:**

Block 4

Date:	Location:	Weapon:	Sites:	Ammo:
Under Par: Y / N	Under Par: Y / N	Under Par: Y / N	Under Par: Y / N	Notes:
Rep 1 Time:	Rep 2 Time:	Rep 3 Time:	Rep 4 Time:	
Rep 1 Score:	Rep 2 Score:	Rep 3 Score:	Rep 4 Score:	**Total Score:**

HAMMER TIME

Date:	Location:	Weapon:	Sites:	Ammo:	
Under Par: Y / N	Under Par: Y / N	Under Par: Y / N	Under Par: Y / N	Notes:	
Rep 1 Time:	Rep 2 Time:	Rep 3 Time:	Rep 4 Time:		
Rep 1 Score:	Rep 2 Score:	Rep 3 Score:	Rep 4 Score:	**Total Score:**	
Date:	Location:	Weapon:	Sites:	Ammo:	
Under Par: Y / N	Under Par: Y / N	Under Par: Y / N	Under Par: Y / N	Notes:	
Rep 1 Time:	Rep 2 Time:	Rep 3 Time:	Rep 4 Time:		
Rep 1 Score:	Rep 2 Score:	Rep 3 Score:	Rep 4 Score:	**Total Score:**	
Date:	Location:	Weapon:	Sites:	Ammo:	
Under Par: Y / N	Under Par: Y / N	Under Par: Y / N	Under Par: Y / N	Notes:	
Rep 1 Time:	Rep 2 Time:	Rep 3 Time:	Rep 4 Time:		
Rep 1 Score:	Rep 2 Score:	Rep 3 Score:	Rep 4 Score:	**Total Score:**	
Date:	Location:	Weapon:	Sites:	Ammo:	
Under Par: Y / N	Under Par: Y / N	Under Par: Y / N	Under Par: Y / N	Notes:	
Rep 1 Time:	Rep 2 Time:	Rep 3 Time:	Rep 4 Time:		
Rep 1 Score:	Rep 2 Score:	Rep 3 Score:	Rep 4 Score:	**Total Score:**	

EXTENSION

Purpose: Increase pistol shot speed at presentation.

Distance: 5 Yards.

Target: GF-1

Par Time: 1 Second.

Extra Equipment Needed: Shot timer.

Rounds Fired Per Rep: 1 Round.   **Total Rounds Fired:** 10 Rounds.

Point Penalty: As per target score.

Repetitions: 10 Reps.

Starting Position & Condition: Ending position of Draw 2 drill (compressed ready). Condition 1.

Description: On the timer beep, press the pistol out in front of you bring it up in line with your eye to a point where you are aiming at the spot on your target. When your pistol reaches the end of the presentation; press the trigger and fire a shot. Firing quickly while getting a flash sight picture of your front sight is the purpose of this drill.

Goals: Novice: 70 Points.   Expert: 90Points.   Gunfighter: 100 Points.

EXTENSION

Date:	Location:	Weapon:	Sights:
Shots over par:	# Outside:	# of 8's:	Notes:
# of 9's:	# of 10's:	**Total Score:** **X's:**	

Date:	Location:	Weapon:	Sights:
Shots over par:	# Outside:	# of 8's:	Notes:
# of 9's:	# of 10's:	**Total Score:** **X's:**	

Date:	Location:	Weapon:	Sights:
Shots over par:	# Outside:	# of 8's:	Notes:
# of 9's:	# of 10's:	**Total Score:** **X's:**	

Date:	Location:	Weapon:	Sights:
Shots over par:	# Outside:	# of 8's:	Notes:
# of 9's:	# of 10's:	**Total Score:** **X's:**	

Date:	Location:	Weapon:	Sights:
Shots over par:	# Outside:	# of 8's:	Notes:
# of 9's:	# of 10's:	**Total Score:** **X's:**	

Date:	Location:	# of 10's:	# of 9's:
	Weapon:	# Outside:	Shots over par:
Sights:		# of 8's:	Notes:
		Total Score:	X's:

Date:	Location:	# of 10's:	# of 9's:
Sights:	Weapon:	# Outside:	Shots over par:
		# of 8's:	Notes:
		Total Score:	X's:

Date:	Location:	# of 10's:	# of 9's:
Sights:	Weapon:	# Outside:	Shots over par:
		# of 8's:	Notes:
		Total Score:	X's:

Date:	Location:	# of 10's:	# of 9's:
Sights:	Weapon:	# Outside:	Shots over par:
		# of 8's:	Notes:
		Total Score:	X's:

Date:	Location:	# of 10's:	# of 9's:
Sights:	Weapon:	# Outside:	Shots over par:
		# of 8's:	Notes:
		Total Score:	X's:

EXTENSION

Date:	Location:	Weapon:	Sights:
Shots over par:	# Outside:	# of 8's:	Notes:
# of 9's:	# of 10's:	**Total Score:** **X's:**	

Date:	Location:	Weapon:	Sights:
Shots over par:	# Outside:	# of 8's:	Notes:
# of 9's:	# of 10's:	**Total Score:** **X's:**	

Date:	Location:	Weapon:	Sights:
Shots over par:	# Outside:	# of 8's:	Notes:
# of 9's:	# of 10's:	**Total Score:** **X's:**	

Date:	Location:	Weapon:	Sights:
Shots over par:	# Outside:	# of 8's:	Notes:
# of 9's:	# of 10's:	**Total Score:** **X's:**	

Date:	Location:	Weapon:	Sights:
Shots over par:	# Outside:	# of 8's:	Notes:
# of 9's:	# of 10's:	**Total Score:** **X's:**	

EXTENSION

Date:	Location:	Weapon:	Sights:
Shots over par:	# Outside:	# of 8's:	Notes:
# of 9's:	# of 10's:	**Total Score:** **X's:**	

Date:	Location:	Weapon:	Sights:
Shots over par:	# Outside:	# of 8's:	Notes:
# of 9's:	# of 10's:	**Total Score:** **X's:**	

Date:	Location:	Weapon:	Sights:
Shots over par:	# Outside:	# of 8's:	Notes:
# of 9's:	# of 10's:	**Total Score:** **X's:**	

Date:	Location:	Weapon:	Sights:
Shots over par:	# Outside:	# of 8's:	Notes:
# of 9's:	# of 10's:	**Total Score:** **X's:**	

Date:	Location:	Weapon:	Sights:
Shots over par:	# Outside:	# of 8's:	Notes:
# of 9's:	# of 10's:	**Total Score:** **X's:**	

EXTENSION

Date:	Location:	Weapon:	Sights:
Shots over par:	# Outside:	# of 8's:	Notes:
# of 9's:	# of 10's:	**Total Score:** **X's:**	

Date:	Location:	Weapon:	Sights:
Shots over par:	# Outside:	# of 8's:	Notes:
# of 9's:	# of 10's:	**Total Score:** **X's:**	

Date:	Location:	Weapon:	Sights:
Shots over par:	# Outside:	# of 8's:	Notes:
# of 9's:	# of 10's:	**Total Score:** **X's:**	

Date:	Location:	Weapon:	Sights:
Shots over par:	# Outside:	# of 8's:	Notes:
# of 9's:	# of 10's:	**Total Score:** **X's:**	

Date:	Location:	Weapon:	Sights:
Shots over par:	# Outside:	# of 8's:	Notes:
# of 9's:	# of 10's:	**Total Score:** **X's:**	

HICKOK

By: Kevin Lippert of Jericho Defense .

Purpose: Increase accuracy and pistol draw speed.

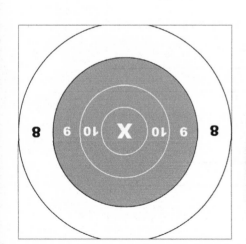

Target: GF-1

Distance: 7 Yards.

Par Time: 2 Seconds.

Extra Equipment Needed: Shot timer.

Rounds Fired Per Rep: 1 Round.   **Total Rounds Fired:** 10 Rounds.

Point Penalty: As per target score.

Repetitions: 10 Reps.

Starting Position & Condition: Standing - Surrender / Interview. Condition 1.

Description: At the timer beep, draw and fire 1 round into the target. At the end of the ten repetitions, count up your score. As you perform your draws, be quick but try to be smooth and deliberate.

Goals: Novice: 70 Points.   **Expert:** 90 Points.   **Gunfighter:** 100 Points.

HICKOK

Date:	Location:	Weapon:	Sights:
Shots over par:	# Outside:	# of 8's:	Notes:
# of 9's:	# of 10's:	**Total Score:** **X's:**	

Date:	Location:	Weapon:	Sights:
Shots over par:	# Outside:	# of 8's:	Notes:
# of 9's:	# of 10's:	**Total Score:** **X's:**	

Date:	Location:	Weapon:	Sights:
Shots over par:	# Outside:	# of 8's:	Notes:
# of 9's:	# of 10's:	**Total Score:** **X's:**	

Date:	Location:	Weapon:	Sights:
Shots over par:	# Outside:	# of 8's:	Notes:
# of 9's:	# of 10's:	**Total Score:** **X's:**	

Date:	Location:	Weapon:	Sights:
Shots over par:	# Outside:	# of 8's:	Notes:
# of 9's:	# of 10's:	**Total Score:** **X's:**	

HICKOK

Date:	Location:	Weapon:	Sights:
Shots over par:	# Outside:	# of 8's:	Notes:
# of 9's:	# of 10's:	**Total Score:** X's:	

Date:	Location:	Weapon:	Sights:
Shots over par:	# Outside:	# of 8's:	Notes:
# of 9's:	# of 10's:	**Total Score:** X's:	

Date:	Location:	Weapon:	Sights:
Shots over par:	# Outside:	# of 8's:	Notes:
# of 9's:	# of 10's:	**Total Score:** X's:	

Date:	Location:	Weapon:	Sights:
Shots over par:	# Outside:	# of 8's:	Notes:
# of 9's:	# of 10's:	**Total Score:** X's:	

Date:	Location:	Weapon:	Sights:
Shots over par:	# Outside:	# of 8's:	Notes:
# of 9's:	# of 10's:	**Total Score:** X's:	

HICKOK

Date:	Location:	Weapon:	Sights:
Shots over par:	# Outside:	# of 8's:	Notes:
# of 9's:	# of 10's:	**Total Score:** **X's:**	

Date:	Location:	Weapon:	Sights:
Shots over par:	# Outside:	# of 8's:	Notes:
# of 9's:	# of 10's:	**Total Score:** **X's:**	

Date:	Location:	Weapon:	Sights:
Shots over par:	# Outside:	# of 8's:	Notes:
# of 9's:	# of 10's:	**Total Score:** **X's:**	

Date:	Location:	Weapon:	Sights:
Shots over par:	# Outside:	# of 8's:	Notes:
# of 9's:	# of 10's:	**Total Score:** **X's:**	

Date:	Location:	Weapon:	Sights:
Shots over par:	# Outside:	# of 8's:	Notes:
# of 9's:	# of 10's:	**Total Score:** **X's:**	

HICKOK

# of 9's:	# of 10's:	Total Score:	X's:
Shots over par:	# Outside:	# of 8's:	Notes:
Date:	Location:	Weapon:	Sights:

# of 9's:	# of 10's:	Total Score:	X's:
Shots over par:	# Outside:	# of 8's:	Notes:
Date:	Location:	Weapon:	Sights:

# of 9's:	# of 10's:	Total Score:	X's:
Shots over par:	# Outside:	# of 8's:	Notes:
Date:	Location:	Weapon:	Sights:

# of 9's:	# of 10's:	Total Score:	X's:
Shots over par:	# Outside:	# of 8's:	Notes:
Date:	Location:	Weapon:	Sights:

# of 9's:	# of 10's:	Total Score:	X's:
Shots over par:	# Outside:	# of 8's:	Notes:
Date:	Location:	Weapon:	Sights:

HICKOK

Date:	Location:	Weapon:	Sights:
Shots over par:	# Outside:	# of 8's:	Notes:
# of 9's:	# of 10's:	**Total Score:** **X's:**	

Date:	Location:	Weapon:	Sights:
Shots over par:	# Outside:	# of 8's:	Notes:
# of 9's:	# of 10's:	**Total Score:** **X's:**	

Date:	Location:	Weapon:	Sights:
Shots over par:	# Outside:	# of 8's:	Notes:
# of 9's:	# of 10's:	**Total Score:** **X's:**	

Date:	Location:	Weapon:	Sights:
Shots over par:	# Outside:	# of 8's:	Notes:
# of 9's:	# of 10's:	**Total Score:** **X's:**	

Date:	Location:	Weapon:	Sights:
Shots over par:	# Outside:	# of 8's:	Notes:
# of 9's:	# of 10's:	**Total Score:** **X's:**	

WILD WEST

Purpose: Increase pistol draw speed and recoil management.

Distance: 10 Yards.

Target: JD-QUAL.

Extra Equipment Needed: Shot timer.

Rounds Fired Per Rep: 2 to 5 Rounds (shooters choice).   **Total Rounds Fired:** 10 to 25 Rounds.

Point Penalty: As per target score.

Repetitions: 5 Reps.

Starting Position & Condition: Standing - Surrender / Interview. Condition 1.

Description: At the timer beep, draw and fire 2 to 5 rounds (shooters choice) into the (5 point) A Zone body box. Record the time. Repeat 5 times and make sure to fire the same number of rounds in each repetition for this session. Remove the high and low times and average the remaining times for an average. Add up your round hit score according to the target scoring and record.

Goals: Focus on cadence with all 5 shots center mass in body A zone box.

Variations: Try different round counts on different sessions and over time see if your average times for the same round counts are coming down and your scoring points are increasing.

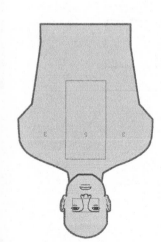

WILD WEST

Date:	Location:	Weapon:	Sights:	A Box: Head / Body
Rep 1 Time:	Rep 2 Time:	Rep 3 Time:	Rep 4 Time:	Rep 5 Time:
1st Shot Time:	1st Shot Time:	1st Shot Time:	1st Shot Time:	1st Shot Time:
# of Shots:	# of Shots:	# of Shots:	# of Shots:	# of Shots:
Ave 1st Shot Time:		**Ave Total Rep Time:**		Notes:

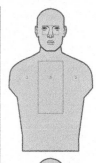

Date:	Location:	Weapon:	Sights:	A Box: Head / Body
Rep 1 Time:	Rep 2 Time:	Rep 3 Time:	Rep 4 Time:	Rep 5 Time:
1st Shot Time:	1st Shot Time:	1st Shot Time:	1st Shot Time:	1st Shot Time:
# of Shots:	# of Shots:	# of Shots:	# of Shots:	# of Shots:
Ave 1st Shot Time:		**Ave Total Rep Time:**		Notes:

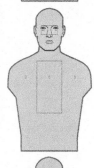

Date:	Location:	Weapon:	Sights:	A Box: Head / Body
Rep 1 Time:	Rep 2 Time:	Rep 3 Time:	Rep 4 Time:	Rep 5 Time:
1st Shot Time:	1st Shot Time:	1st Shot Time:	1st Shot Time:	1st Shot Time:
# of Shots::	# of Shots:	# of Shots:	# of Shots:	# of Shots:
Ave 1st Shot Time:		**Ave Total Rep Time:**		Notes:

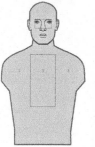

WILD WEST

Date:	Location:	Weapon:	Sights:	A Box: Head / Body
Rep 1 Time:	Rep 2 Time:	Rep 3 Time:	Rep 4 Time:	Rep 5 Time:
1st Shot Time:	1st Shot Time:	1st Shot Time:	1st Shot Time:	1st Shot Time:
# of Shots:	# of Shots:	# of Shots:	# of Shots:	# of Shots:
Ave 1st Shot Time:		Ave Total Rep Time:		Notes:

Date:	Location:	Weapon:	Sights:	A Box: Head / Body
Rep 1 Time:	Rep 2 Time:	Rep 3 Time:	Rep 4 Time:	Rep 5 Time:
1st Shot Time:	1st Shot Time:	1st Shot Time:	1st Shot Time:	1st Shot Time:
# of Shots:	# of Shots:	# of Shots:	# of Shots:	# of Shots:
Ave 1st Shot Time:		Ave Total Rep Time:		Notes:

Date:	Location:	Weapon:	Sights:	A Box: Head / Body
Rep 1 Time:	Rep 2 Time:	Rep 3 Time:	Rep 4 Time:	Rep 5 Time:
1st Shot Time:	1st Shot Time:	1st Shot Time:	1st Shot Time:	1st Shot Time:
# of Shots::	# of Shots:	# of Shots:	# of Shots:	# of Shots:
Ave 1st Shot Time:		Ave Total Rep Time:		Notes:

WILD WEST

Date:	Location:	Weapon:	Sights:	A Box: Head / Body
Rep 1 Time:	Rep 2 Time:	Rep 3 Time:	Rep 4 Time:	Rep 5 Time:
1st Shot Time:	1st Shot Time:	1st Shot Time:	1st Shot Time:	1st Shot Time:
# of Shots:	# of Shots:	# of Shots:	# of Shots:	# of Shots:
Ave 1st Shot Time:		**Ave Total Rep Time:**		Notes:

Date:	Location:	Weapon:	Sights:	A Box: Head / Body
Rep 1 Time:	Rep 2 Time:	Rep 3 Time:	Rep 4 Time:	Rep 5 Time:
1st Shot Time:	1st Shot Time:	1st Shot Time:	1st Shot Time:	1st Shot Time:
# of Shots:	# of Shots:	# of Shots:	# of Shots:	# of Shots:
Ave 1st Shot Time:		**Ave Total Rep Time:**		Notes:

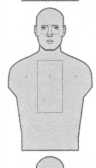

Date:	Location:	Weapon:	Sights:	A Box: Head / Body
Rep 1 Time:	Rep 2 Time:	Rep 3 Time:	Rep 4 Time:	Rep 5 Time:
1st Shot Time:	1st Shot Time:	1st Shot Time:	1st Shot Time:	1st Shot Time:
# of Shots::	# of Shots:	# of Shots:	# of Shots:	# of Shots:
Ave 1st Shot Time:		**Ave Total Rep Time:**		Notes:

WILD WEST

Date:	Location:	Weapon:	Sights:	A Box: Head / Body
Rep 1 Time:	Rep 2 Time:	Rep 3 Time:	Rep 4 Time:	Rep 5 Time:
1st Shot Time:	1st Shot Time:	1st Shot Time:	1st Shot Time:	1st Shot Time:
# of Shots:	# of Shots:	# of Shots:	# of Shots:	# of Shots:
Ave 1st Shot Time:		Ave Total Rep Time:		Notes:

Date:	Location:	Weapon:	Sights:	A Box: Head / Body
Rep 1 Time:	Rep 2 Time:	Rep 3 Time:	Rep 4 Time:	Rep 5 Time:
1st Shot Time:	1st Shot Time:	1st Shot Time:	1st Shot Time:	1st Shot Time:
# of Shots:	# of Shots:	# of Shots:	# of Shots:	# of Shots:
Ave 1st Shot Time:		Ave Total Rep Time:		Notes:

Date:	Location:	Weapon:	Sights:	A Box: Head / Body
Rep 1 Time:	Rep 2 Time:	Rep 3 Time:	Rep 4 Time:	Rep 5 Time:
1st Shot Time:	1st Shot Time:	1st Shot Time:	1st Shot Time:	1st Shot Time:
# of Shots:	# of Shots:	# of Shots:	# of Shots:	# of Shots:
Ave 1st Shot Time:		Ave Total Rep Time:		Notes:

WILD WEST

Date:	Location:	Weapon:	Sights:	A Box: Head / Body
Rep 1 Time:	Rep 2 Time:	Rep 3 Time:	Rep 4 Time:	Rep 5 Time:
1st Shot Time:	1st Shot Time:	1st Shot Time:	1st Shot Time:	1st Shot Time:
# of Shots:	# of Shots:	# of Shots:	# of Shots:	# of Shots:
Ave 1st Shot Time:		**Ave Total Rep Time:**		Notes:

Date:	Location:	Weapon:	Sights:	A Box: Head / Body
Rep 1 Time:	Rep 2 Time:	Rep 3 Time:	Rep 4 Time:	Rep 5 Time:
1st Shot Time:	1st Shot Time:	1st Shot Time:	1st Shot Time:	1st Shot Time:
# of Shots:	# of Shots:	# of Shots:	# of Shots:	# of Shots:
Ave 1st Shot Time:		**Ave Total Rep Time:**		Notes:

Date:	Location:	Weapon:	Sights:	A Box: Head / Body
Rep 1 Time:	Rep 2 Time:	Rep 3 Time:	Rep 4 Time:	Rep 5 Time:
1st Shot Time:	1st Shot Time:	1st Shot Time:	1st Shot Time:	1st Shot Time:
# of Shots::	# of Shots:	# of Shots:	# of Shots:	# of Shots:
Ave 1st Shot Time:		**Ave Total Rep Time:**		Notes:

COLLATERAL

Purpose: Pistol draw speed and quick shot cadence.

Distance: 3 & 5 Yards.

Target: JD-QUAL1 X 2. Position the targets 3 feet apart at 3 and 5 yards.

Par Time: 3 Seconds.

Extra Equipment Needed: Shot timer.

Rounds Fired Per Rep: 4 Rounds.   **Total Rounds Fired:** 12 Rounds.

Point Penalty: As per target score.

Repetitions: 3 Reps.

Starting Position & Condition: Standing - Surrender / Interview. Condition 1.

Description: At the timer beep, draw and fire 2 rounds per target starting with the 3 yard target then transition to the 5 yard target. Record time, score targets. For every hit in the 3 scoring zone, add 2 seconds to your time. For every hit in the 0 scoring zone, add 5 seconds to your time. Add the penalty time onto your recorded time for that repetition. Average all of the repetitions and there is your time. The more accurate you become, the more your time will come down.

Goals: The goal is within the par time and zero added seconds.

Variations: Try head A zones for added difficulty.

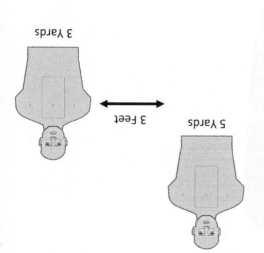

3 Yards

3 Feet

5 Yards

COLLATERAL

Date:	Location:	Weapon:	A Box: Head / Body
Rep 1 Time:	Rep 2 Time:	Rep 3 Time:	Notes:
+ Penalties:	+ Penalties:	+ Penalties:	
= Rep 1 Score:	= Rep 2 Score:	= Rep 3 Score:	**Average Rep Score:**

Date:	Location:	Weapon:	A Box: Head / Body
Rep 1 Time:	Rep 2 Time:	Rep 3 Time:	Notes:
+ Penalties:	+ Penalties:	+ Penalties:	
= Rep 1 Score:	= Rep 2 Score:	= Rep 3 Score:	**Average Rep Score:**

Date:	Location:	Weapon:	A Box: Head / Body
Rep 1 Time:	Rep 2 Time:	Rep 3 Time:	Notes:
+ Penalties:	+ Penalties:	+ Penalties:	
= Rep 1 Score:	= Rep 2 Score:	= Rep 3 Score:	**Average Rep Score:**

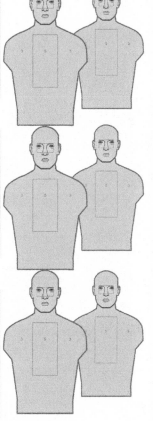

COLLATERAL

Date:	Location:	Weapon:	A Box: Head / Body
Rep 1 Time:	Rep 2 Time:	Rep 3 Time:	Notes:
+ Penalties:	+ Penalties:	+ Penalties:	
= Rep 1 Score:	= Rep 2 Score:	= Rep 3 Score:	**Average Rep Score:**

Date:	Location:	Weapon:	A Box: Head / Body
Rep 1 Time:	Rep 2 Time:	Rep 3 Time:	Notes:
+ Penalties:	+ Penalties:	+ Penalties:	
= Rep 1 Score:	= Rep 2 Score:	= Rep 3 Score:	**Average Rep Score:**

Date:	Location:	Weapon:	A Box: Head / Body
Rep 1 Time:	Rep 2 Time:	Rep 3 Time:	Notes:
+ Penalties:	+ Penalties:	+ Penalties:	
= Rep 1 Score:	= Rep 2 Score:	= Rep 3 Score:	**Average Rep Score:**

COLLATERAL

Date:	Location:	Weapon:	A Box: Head / Body
Rep 1 Time:	Rep 2 Time:	Rep 3 Time:	Notes:
+ Penalties:	+ Penalties:	+ Penalties:	
= Rep 1 Score:	= Rep 2 Score:	= Rep 3 Score:	**Average Rep Score:**

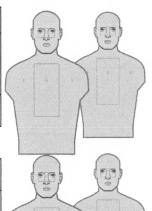

Date:	Location:	Weapon:	A Box: Head / Body
Rep 1 Time:	Rep 2 Time:	Rep 3 Time:	Notes:
+ Penalties:	+ Penalties:	+ Penalties:	
= Rep 1 Score:	= Rep 2 Score:	= Rep 3 Score:	**Average Rep Score:**

Date:	Location:	Weapon:	A Box: Head / Body
Rep 1 Time:	Rep 2 Time:	Rep 3 Time:	Notes:
+ Penalties:	+ Penalties:	+ Penalties:	
= Rep 1 Score:	= Rep 2 Score:	= Rep 3 Score:	**Average Rep Score:**

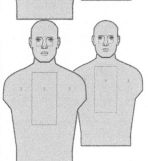

RECOIL

Purpose: Recoil management with multiple targets.

Distance: 10 Yards.

Target: JD-QUAL1 X 2. Position 2 targets set up 5 feet apart at 10 yards.

Par Time: 4.3 Seconds.

Extra Equipment Needed: Shot timer.

Rounds Fired Per Rep: 8 Rounds.   **Total Rounds Fired:** 24 Rounds.

Point Penalty: As per target score.

Repetitions: 3 Reps.

Starting Position & Condition: Standing - Surrender / Interview. Condition 1.

Description: At the timer beep, draw, fire 4 rounds into the A Zone (5 point) body box, transition to next target and fire 4 rounds into the A Zone (5 point) body box.

Goals: The goal is par time and 120 points.

Variations: Try head A zones for added difficulty.

5 Feet

RECOIL

Date:	Location:	Weapon:	A Box: Head / Body
Rep 1 Time:	Rep 2 Time:	Rep 3 Time:	Notes:
Under Par: Y / N	Under Par: Y / N	Under Par: Y / N	
Rep 1 Score:	Rep 2 Score:	Rep 3 Score:	**Total Score:**

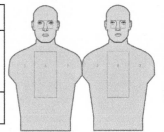

Date:	Location:	Weapon:	A Box: Head / Body
Rep 1 Time:	Rep 2 Time:	Rep 3 Time:	Notes:
Under Par: Y / N	Under Par: Y / N	Under Par: Y / N	
Rep 1 Score:	Rep 2 Score:	Rep 3 Score:	**Total Score:**

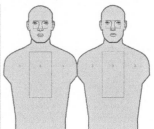

Date:	Location:	Weapon:	A Box: Head / Body
Rep 1 Time:	Rep 2 Time:	Rep 3 Time:	Notes:
Under Par: Y / N	Under Par: Y / N	Under Par: Y / N	
Rep 1 Score:	Rep 2 Score:	Rep 3 Score:	**Total Score:**

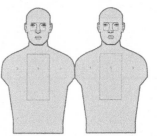

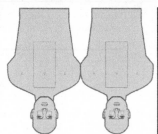

Date:	Location:	Weapon:	A Box: Head / Body
Rep 1 Time:	Rep 2 Time:	Rep 3 Time:	Notes:
Under Par: Y / N	Under Par: Y / N	Under Par: Y / N	
Rep 1 Score:	Rep 2 Score:	Rep 3 Score:	**Total Score:**

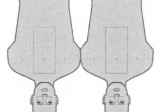

Date:	Location:	Weapon:	A Box: Head / Body
Rep 1 Time:	Rep 2 Time:	Rep 3 Time:	Notes:
Under Par: Y / N	Under Par: Y / N	Under Par: Y / N	
Rep 1 Score:	Rep 2 Score:	Rep 3 Score:	**Total Score:**

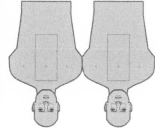

Date:	Location:	Weapon:	A Box: Head / Body
Rep 1 Time:	Rep 2 Time:	Rep 3 Time:	Notes:
Under Par: Y / N	Under Par: Y / N	Under Par: Y / N	
Rep 1 Score:	Rep 2 Score:	Rep 3 Score:	**Total Score:**

RECOIL

Date:	Location:	Weapon:	A Box: Head / Body
Rep 1 Time:	Rep 2 Time:	Rep 3 Time:	Notes:
Under Par: Y / N	Under Par: Y / N	Under Par: Y / N	
Rep 1 Score:	Rep 2 Score:	Rep 3 Score:	**Total Score:**

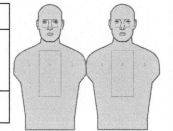

Date:	Location:	Weapon:	A Box: Head / Body
Rep 1 Time:	Rep 2 Time:	Rep 3 Time:	Notes:
Under Par: Y / N	Under Par: Y / N	Under Par: Y / N	
Rep 1 Score:	Rep 2 Score:	Rep 3 Score:	**Total Score:**

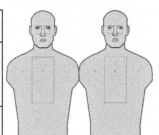

Date:	Location:	Weapon:	A Box: Head / Body
Rep 1 Time:	Rep 2 Time:	Rep 3 Time:	Notes:
Under Par: Y / N	Under Par: Y / N	Under Par: Y / N	
Rep 1 Score:	Rep 2 Score:	Rep 3 Score:	**Total Score:**

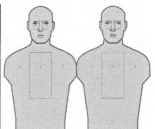

RECOIL

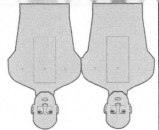

Date:	Location:	Weapon:	A Box: Head / Body
Rep 1 Time:	Rep 2 Time:	Rep 3 Time:	Notes:
Under Par: Y / N	Under Par: Y / N	Under Par: Y / N	
Rep 1 Score:	Rep 2 Score:	Rep 3 Score:	**Total Score:**

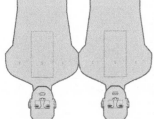

Date:	Location:	Weapon:	A Box: Head / Body
Rep 1 Time:	Rep 2 Time:	Rep 3 Time:	Notes:
Under Par: Y / N	Under Par: Y / N	Under Par: Y / N	
Rep 1 Score:	Rep 2 Score:	Rep 3 Score:	**Total Score:**

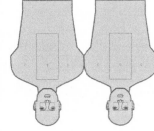

Date:	Location:	Weapon:	A Box: Head / Body
Rep 1 Time:	Rep 2 Time:	Rep 3 Time:	Notes:
Under Par: Y / N	Under Par: Y / N	Under Par: Y / N	
Rep 1 Score:	Rep 2 Score:	Rep 3 Score:	**Total Score:**

RECOIL

Date:	Location:	Weapon:	A Box: Head / Body
Rep 1 Time:	Rep 2 Time:	Rep 3 Time:	Notes:
Under Par: Y / N	Under Par: Y / N	Under Par: Y / N	
Rep 1 Score:	Rep 2 Score:	Rep 3 Score:	**Total Score:**

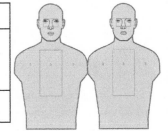

Date:	Location:	Weapon:	A Box: Head / Body
Rep 1 Time:	Rep 2 Time:	Rep 3 Time:	Notes:
Under Par: Y / N	Under Par: Y / N	Under Par: Y / N	
Rep 1 Score:	Rep 2 Score:	Rep 3 Score:	**Total Score:**

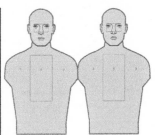

Date:	Location:	Weapon:	A Box: Head / Body
Rep 1 Time:	Rep 2 Time:	Rep 3 Time:	Notes:
Under Par: Y / N	Under Par: Y / N	Under Par: Y / N	
Rep 1 Score:	Rep 2 Score:	Rep 3 Score:	**Total Score:**

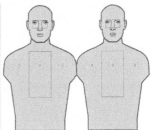

IN THE WEEDS

Purpose: Accuracy with multiple targets.

Distance: 10, 20, 35 Yards.

Target: JD-QUAL1 X 3. Position the targets 5 feet apart at 10, 20 and 35 yards.

Extra Equipment Needed: Shot timer.

Rounds Fired Per Rep: 9 Rounds.   **Total Rounds Fired:** 27 Rounds.

Point Penalty: As per target score.

Repetitions: 3 Reps.

Starting Position & Condition: Standing - Low Ready. Condition 1.

Description: At the timer beep, fire 3 rounds per target. Record time and score targets. For every hit in the 3 scoring zone, add 2 seconds to your time. For every hit in the 0 scoring zone, add 5 seconds to your time. Add the penalty time onto your recorded time for that repetition. Average all of the repetitions and there is your time.

Goals: Beat your personal best time.

Variations: Try shooting this drill from front to back or back to front in different practice sessions and see what your time differences are.

35 Yards

5 Feet

20 Yards

5 Feet

10 Yards

IN THE WEEDS

Date:	Location:	Weapon:	Near to Far / Far to Near	
Rep 1 Time:	Rep 2 Time:	Rep 3 Time:	Notes:	
+ Penalties:	+ Penalties:	+ Penalties:		
= Rep 1 Score:	= Rep 2 Score:	= Rep 3 Score:	**Ave Rep Score:**	

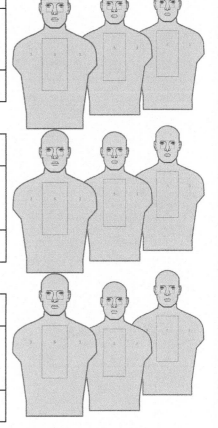

Date:	Location:	Weapon:	Near to Far / Far to Near
Rep 1 Time:	Rep 2 Time:	Rep 3 Time:	Notes:
+ Penalties:	+ Penalties:	+ Penalties:	
= Rep 1 Score:	= Rep 2 Score:	= Rep 3 Score:	**Ave Rep Score:**

Date:	Location:	Weapon:	Near to Far / Far to Near
Rep 1 Time:	Rep 2 Time:	Rep 3 Time:	Notes:
+ Penalties:	+ Penalties:	+ Penalties:	
= Rep 1 Score:	= Rep 2 Score:	= Rep 3 Score:	**Ave Rep Score:**

IN THE WEEDS

Date:	Location:	Weapon:	Near to Far / Far to Near	
Rep 1 Time:	Rep 2 Time:	Rep 3 Time:	Notes:	
+ Penalties:	+ Penalties:	+ Penalties:		
= Rep 1 Score:	= Rep 2 Score:	= Rep 3 Score:	**Ave Rep Score:**	

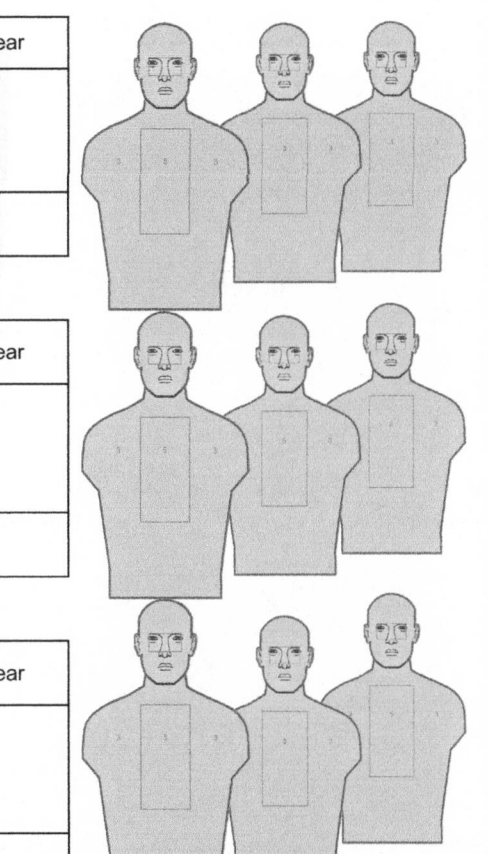

Date:	Location:	Weapon:	Near to Far / Far to Near	
Rep 1 Time:	Rep 2 Time:	Rep 3 Time:	Notes:	
+ Penalties:	+ Penalties:	+ Penalties:		
= Rep 1 Score:	= Rep 2 Score:	= Rep 3 Score:	**Ave Rep Score:**	

Date:	Location:	Weapon:	Near to Far / Far to Near	
Rep 1 Time:	Rep 2 Time:	Rep 3 Time:	Notes:	
+ Penalties:	+ Penalties:	+ Penalties:		
= Rep 1 Score:	= Rep 2 Score:	= Rep 3 Score:	**Ave Rep Score:**	

IN THE WEEDS

Date:	Location:	Weapon:	Near to Far / Far to Near
Rep 1 Time:	Rep 2 Time:	Rep 3 Time:	Notes:
+ Penalties:	+ Penalties:	+ Penalties:	
= Rep 1 Score:	= Rep 2 Score:	= Rep 3 Score:	**Ave Rep Score:**

Date:	Location:	Weapon:	Near to Far / Far to Near
Rep 1 Time:	Rep 2 Time:	Rep 3 Time:	Notes:
+ Penalties:	+ Penalties:	+ Penalties:	
= Rep 1 Score:	= Rep 2 Score:	= Rep 3 Score:	**Ave Rep Score:**

Date:	Location:	Weapon:	Near to Far / Far to Near
Rep 1 Time:	Rep 2 Time:	Rep 3 Time:	Notes:
+ Penalties:	+ Penalties:	+ Penalties:	
= Rep 1 Score:	= Rep 2 Score:	= Rep 3 Score:	**Ave Rep Score:**

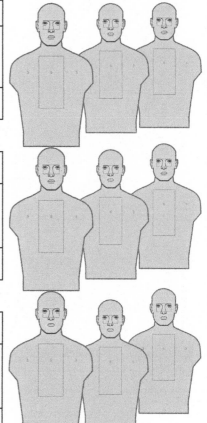

IN THE WEEDS

Date:	Location:	Weapon:	Near to Far / Far to Near
Rep 1 Time:	Rep 2 Time:	Rep 3 Time:	Notes:
+ Penalties:	+ Penalties:	+ Penalties:	
= Rep 1 Score:	= Rep 2 Score:	= Rep 3 Score:	**Ave Rep Score:**

Date:	Location:	Weapon:	Near to Far / Far to Near
Rep 1 Time:	Rep 2 Time:	Rep 3 Time:	Notes:
+ Penalties:	+ Penalties:	+ Penalties:	
= Rep 1 Score:	= Rep 2 Score:	= Rep 3 Score:	**Ave Rep Score:**

Date:	Location:	Weapon:	Near to Far / Far to Near
Rep 1 Time:	Rep 2 Time:	Rep 3 Time:	Notes:
+ Penalties:	+ Penalties:	+ Penalties:	
= Rep 1 Score:	= Rep 2 Score:	= Rep 3 Score:	**Ave Rep Score:**

IN THE WEEDS

Date:	Location:	Weapon:	Near to Far / Far to Near
Rep 1 Time:	Rep 2 Time:	Rep 3 Time:	Notes:
+ Penalties:	+ Penalties:	+ Penalties:	
= Rep 1 Score:	= Rep 2 Score:	= Rep 3 Score:	**Ave Rep Score:**

Date:	Location:	Weapon:	Near to Far / Far to Near
Rep 1 Time:	Rep 2 Time:	Rep 3 Time:	Notes:
+ Penalties:	+ Penalties:	+ Penalties:	
= Rep 1 Score:	= Rep 2 Score:	= Rep 3 Score:	**Ave Rep Score:**

Date:	Location:	Weapon:	Near to Far / Far to Near
Rep 1 Time:	Rep 2 Time:	Rep 3 Time:	Notes:
+ Penalties:	+ Penalties:	+ Penalties:	
= Rep 1 Score:	= Rep 2 Score:	= Rep 3 Score:	**Ave Rep Score:**

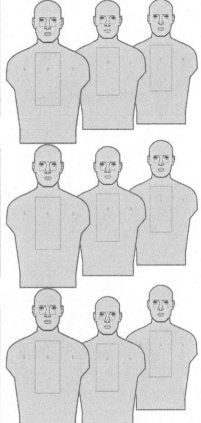

THE OUTLAW JOSEY WALES

Purpose: Speed.

Distance: 5 Yards.

Target: JD-QUAL1 X 3 Position the targets 5 feet apart at 5 yards.

Extra Equipment Needed: Shot timer.

Rounds Fired Per Rep: 3 Rounds.   **Total Rounds Fired:** 9 Rounds.

Point Penalty: As per target score.

Repetitions: 3 Reps.

Starting Position & Condition: Standing - Surrender / Interview. Condition 1.

Description: At the timer beep, draw and fire 1 round per target. Record time. For every hit in the 3 scoring zone, add 2 seconds to your time. For every hit in the 0 scoring zone, add 5 seconds to your time. Add the penalty time onto your recorded time for that repetition. Average all of the repetitions and there is your time. The more accurate you become, the more your time will come down.

Goals: Beat your personal best time.

Variations: Try shooting this drill from left to right or right to left in different practice sessions and see what your time differences are.

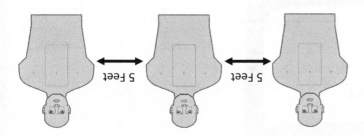

5 Feet   5 Feet

THE OUTLAW JOSEY WALES

Date:	Location:	Weapon:	Left to Right / Right to Left
Rep 1 Time:	Rep 2 Time:	Rep 3 Time:	Notes:
+ Penalties:	+ Penalties:	+ Penalties:	
= Rep 1 Score:	= Rep 2 Score:	= Rep 3 Score:	**Ave Rep Score:**

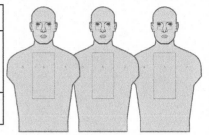

Date:	Location:	Weapon:	Left to Right / Right to Left
Rep 1 Time:	Rep 2 Time:	Rep 3 Time:	Notes:
+ Penalties:	+ Penalties:	+ Penalties:	
= Rep 1 Score:	= Rep 2 Score:	= Rep 3 Score:	**Ave Rep Score:**

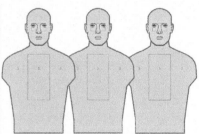

Date:	Location:	Weapon:	Left to Right / Right to Left
Rep 1 Time:	Rep 2 Time:	Rep 3 Time:	Notes:
+ Penalties:	+ Penalties:	+ Penalties:	
= Rep 1 Score:	= Rep 2 Score:	= Rep 3 Score:	**Ave Rep Score:**

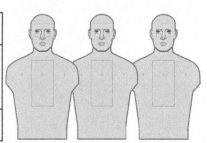

THE OUTLAW JOSEY WALES

Date:	Location:	Weapon:	Left to Right / Right to Left
Rep 1 Time:	Rep 2 Time:	Rep 3 Time:	Notes:
+ Penalties:	+ Penalties:	+ Penalties:	
= Rep 1 Score:	= Rep 2 Score:	= Rep 3 Score:	**Ave Rep Score:**

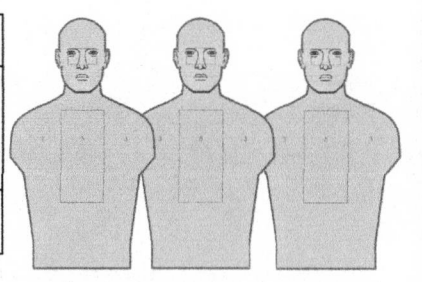

Date:	Location:	Weapon:	Left to Right / Right to Left
Rep 1 Time:	Rep 2 Time:	Rep 3 Time:	Notes:
+ Penalties:	+ Penalties:	+ Penalties:	
= Rep 1 Score:	= Rep 2 Score:	= Rep 3 Score:	**Ave Rep Score:**

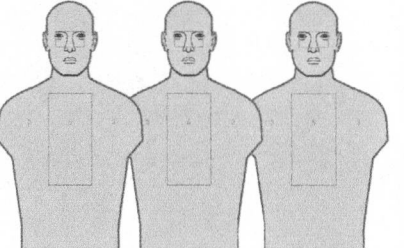

Date:	Location:	Weapon:	Left to Right / Right to Left
Rep 1 Time:	Rep 2 Time:	Rep 3 Time:	Notes:
+ Penalties:	+ Penalties:	+ Penalties:	
= Rep 1 Score:	= Rep 2 Score:	= Rep 3 Score:	**Ave Rep Score:**

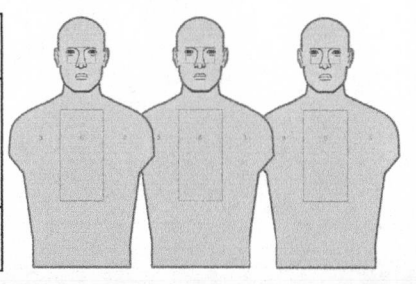

THE OUTLAW JOSEY WALES

Date:	Location:	Weapon:	Left to Right / Right to Left
Rep 1 Time:	Rep 2 Time:	Rep 3 Time:	Notes:
+ Penalties:	+ Penalties:	+ Penalties:	
= Rep 1 Score:	= Rep 2 Score:	= Rep 3 Score:	**Ave Rep Score:**

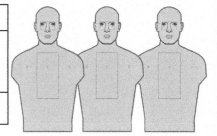

Date:	Location:	Weapon:	Left to Right / Right to Left
Rep 1 Time:	Rep 2 Time:	Rep 3 Time:	Notes:
+ Penalties:	+ Penalties:	+ Penalties:	
= Rep 1 Score:	= Rep 2 Score:	= Rep 3 Score:	**Ave Rep Score:**

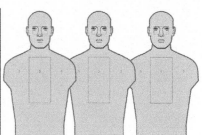

Date:	Location:	Weapon:	Left to Right / Right to Left
Rep 1 Time:	Rep 2 Time:	Rep 3 Time:	Notes:
+ Penalties:	+ Penalties:	+ Penalties:	
= Rep 1 Score:	= Rep 2 Score:	= Rep 3 Score:	**Ave Rep Score:**

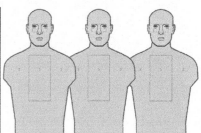

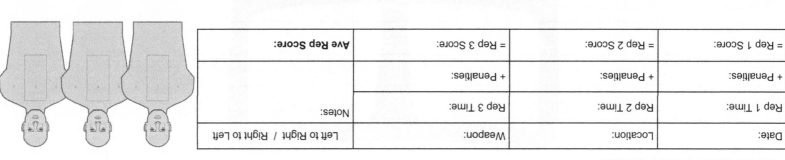

THE OUTLAW JOSEY WALES

Date:	Location:	Weapon:	Left to Right / Right to Left
Rep 1 Time:	Rep 2 Time:	Rep 3 Time:	Notes:
+ Penalties:	+ Penalties:	+ Penalties:	
= Rep 1 Score:	= Rep 2 Score:	= Rep 3 Score:	Ave Rep Score:

Date:	Location:	Weapon:	Left to Right / Right to Left
Rep 1 Time:	Rep 2 Time:	Rep 3 Time:	Notes:
+ Penalties:	+ Penalties:	+ Penalties:	
= Rep 1 Score:	= Rep 2 Score:	= Rep 3 Score:	Ave Rep Score:

Date:	Location:	Weapon:	Left to Right / Right to Left
Rep 1 Time:	Rep 2 Time:	Rep 3 Time:	Notes:
+ Penalties:	+ Penalties:	+ Penalties:	
= Rep 1 Score:	= Rep 2 Score:	= Rep 3 Score:	Ave Rep Score:

THE OUTLAW JOSEY WALES

Date:	Location:	Weapon:	Left to Right / Right to Left	
Rep 1 Time:	Rep 2 Time:	Rep 3 Time:	Notes:	
+ Penalties:	+ Penalties:	+ Penalties:		
= Rep 1 Score:	= Rep 2 Score:	= Rep 3 Score:	**Ave Rep Score:**	

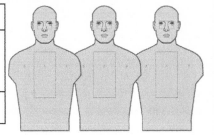

Date:	Location:	Weapon:	Left to Right / Right to Left	
Rep 1 Time:	Rep 2 Time:	Rep 3 Time:	Notes:	
+ Penalties:	+ Penalties:	+ Penalties:		
= Rep 1 Score:	= Rep 2 Score:	= Rep 3 Score:	**Ave Rep Score:**	

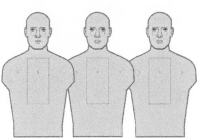

Date:	Location:	Weapon:	Left to Right / Right to Left	
Rep 1 Time:	Rep 2 Time:	Rep 3 Time:	Notes:	
+ Penalties:	+ Penalties:	+ Penalties:		
= Rep 1 Score:	= Rep 2 Score:	= Rep 3 Score:	**Ave Rep Score:**	

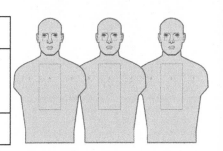

OLD WEST GUN FIGHT

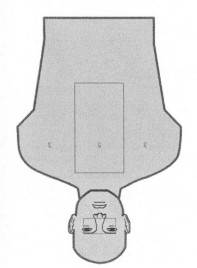

Purpose: Gun fight speed observation.

Distance: 10 Yards.

Target: JD-QUAL1

Par Time: 4 Seconds.

Extra Equipment Needed: Shot timer.

Rounds Fired Per Rep: 5 Rounds.   **Total Rounds Fired:** 15 Rounds.

Point Penalty: See description.

Repetitions: 3 Reps.

Starting Position & Condition: Standing - Surrender / Interview. Condition 1.

Description: Run 50 yards or do 2X25 yard shuttle runs, do 5 push-ups or 15 jumping jacks to get your heart rate up. Immediately afterwards, at the timer beep, step to one side with one step, draw and fire 5 rounds into the (5 point) A Zone body box. Repeat 3 times. Failing to make the par time of 4 seconds or any rounds outside the body box gives a fail for the drill.

Goals: All rounds in A box under par time.

Variations: Double the run and calisthenics once you achieve a perfect score.

OLD WEST GUN FIGHT

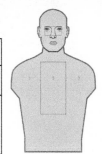

Date:	Location:	Weapon:	Run Distance:
Rep 1 Under Par: Y / N	Rep 2 Under Par: Y / N	Rep 3 Under Par: Y / N	# of exercises:
Total Rep 1 Time:	Total Rep 2 Time:	Total Rep 3 Time:	Notes:
All shots in A Box: Y / N	All shots in A Box: Y / N	All shots in A Box: Y / N	

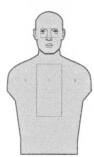

Date:	Location:	Weapon:	Run Distance:
Rep 1 Under Par: Y / N	Rep 2 Under Par: Y / N	Rep 3 Under Par: Y / N	# of exercises:
Total Rep 1 Time:	Total Rep 2 Time:	Total Rep 3 Time:	Notes:
All shots in A Box: Y / N	All shots in A Box: Y / N	All shots in A Box: Y / N	

Date:	Location:	Weapon:	Run Distance:
Rep 1 Under Par: Y / N	Rep 2 Under Par: Y / N	Rep 3 Under Par: Y / N	# of exercises:
Total Rep 1 Time:	Total Rep 2 Time:	Total Rep 3 Time:	Notes:
All shots in A Box: Y / N	All shots in A Box: Y / N	All shots in A Box: Y / N	

OLD WEST GUN FIGHT

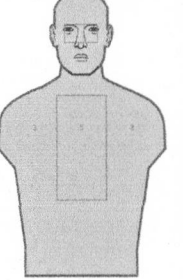

Date:	Location:	Weapon:	Run Distance:
Rep 1 Under Par: Y / N	Rep 2 Under Par: Y / N	Rep 3 Under Par: Y / N	# of exercises:
Total Rep 1 Time:	Total Rep 2 Time:	Total Rep 3 Time:	Notes:
All shots in A Box: Y / N	All shots in A Box: Y / N	All shots in A Box: Y / N	

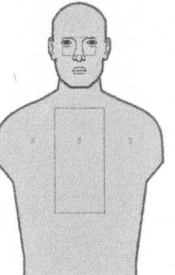

Date:	Location:	Weapon:	Run Distance:
Rep 1 Under Par: Y / N	Rep 2 Under Par: Y / N	Rep 3 Under Par: Y / N	# of exercises:
Total Rep 1 Time:	Total Rep 2 Time:	Total Rep 3 Time:	Notes:
All shots in A Box: Y / N	All shots in A Box: Y / N	All shots in A Box: Y / N	

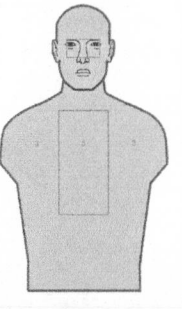

Date:	Location:	Weapon:	Run Distance:
Rep 1 Under Par: Y / N	Rep 2 Under Par: Y / N	Rep 3 Under Par: Y / N	# of exercises:
Total Rep 1 Time:	Total Rep 2 Time:	Total Rep 3 Time:	Notes:
All shots in A Box: Y / N	All shots in A Box: Y / N	All shots in A Box: Y / N	

OLD WEST GUN FIGHT

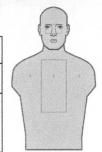

Date:	Location:	Weapon:	Run Distance:
Rep 1 Under Par: Y / N	Rep 2 Under Par: Y / N	Rep 3 Under Par: Y / N	# of exercises:
Total Rep 1 Time:	Total Rep 2 Time:	Total Rep 3 Time:	Notes:
All shots in A Box: Y / N	All shots in A Box: Y / N	All shots in A Box: Y / N	

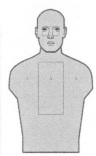

Date:	Location:	Weapon:	Run Distance:
Rep 1 Under Par: Y / N	Rep 2 Under Par: Y / N	Rep 3 Under Par: Y / N	# of exercises:
Total Rep 1 Time:	Total Rep 2 Time:	Total Rep 3 Time:	Notes:
All shots in A Box: Y / N	All shots in A Box: Y / N	All shots in A Box: Y / N	

Date:	Location:	Weapon:	Run Distance:
Rep 1 Under Par: Y / N	Rep 2 Under Par: Y / N	Rep 3 Under Par: Y / N	# of exercises:
Total Rep 1 Time:	Total Rep 2 Time:	Total Rep 3 Time:	Notes:
All shots in A Box: Y / N	All shots in A Box: Y / N	All shots in A Box: Y / N	

OLD WEST GUN FIGHT

Date:	Location:	Weapon:	Run Distance:
Rep 1 Under Par: Y / N	Rep 2 Under Par: Y / N	Rep 3 Under Par: Y / N	# of exercises:
Total Rep 1 Time:	Total Rep 2 Time:	Total Rep 3 Time:	Notes:
All shots in A Box: Y / N	All shots in A Box: Y / N	All shots in A Box: Y / N	

Date:	Location:	Weapon:	Run Distance:
Rep 1 Under Par: Y / N	Rep 2 Under Par: Y / N	Rep 3 Under Par: Y / N	# of exercises:
Total Rep 1 Time:	Total Rep 2 Time:	Total Rep 3 Time:	Notes:
All shots in A Box: Y / N	All shots in A Box: Y / N	All shots in A Box: Y / N	

Date:	Location:	Weapon:	Run Distance:
Rep 1 Under Par: Y / N	Rep 2 Under Par: Y / N	Rep 3 Under Par: Y / N	# of exercises:
Total Rep 1 Time:	Total Rep 2 Time:	Total Rep 3 Time:	Notes:
All shots in A Box: Y / N	All shots in A Box: Y / N	All shots in A Box: Y / N	

OLD WEST GUN FIGHT

Date:	Location:	Weapon:	Run Distance:
Rep 1 Under Par: Y / N	Rep 2 Under Par: Y / N	Rep 3 Under Par: Y / N	# of exercises:
Total Rep 1 Time:	Total Rep 2 Time:	Total Rep 3 Time:	Notes:
All shots in A Box: Y / N	All shots in A Box: Y / N	All shots in A Box: Y / N	

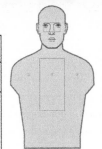

Date:	Location:	Weapon:	Run Distance:
Rep 1 Under Par: Y / N	Rep 2 Under Par: Y / N	Rep 3 Under Par: Y / N	# of exercises:
Total Rep 1 Time:	Total Rep 2 Time:	Total Rep 3 Time:	Notes:
All shots in A Box: Y / N	All shots in A Box: Y / N	All shots in A Box: Y / N	

Date:	Location:	Weapon:	Run Distance:
Rep 1 Under Par: Y / N	Rep 2 Under Par: Y / N	Rep 3 Under Par: Y / N	# of exercises:
Total Rep 1 Time:	Total Rep 2 Time:	Total Rep 3 Time:	Notes:
All shots in A Box: Y / N	All shots in A Box: Y / N	All shots in A Box: Y / N	

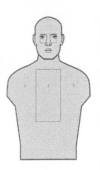

STREET BURNER

Purpose: Multiple pistol skills.

Distance: 15 Yards.

Target: JD-QUAL1 X 2

Par Time: 15 Seconds.

Extra Equipment Needed: Shot timer, roughly 3 foot high barrier, 2 pistol mags, mag pouch.

Rounds Fired Per Rep: 10 Rounds.   **Total Rounds Fired:** 30 Rounds.

Point Penalty: See description.

Repetitions: 3 Reps.

Starting Position & Condition: Standing - Surrender / Interview. Condition 1.

Description: With your pistol holstered in Condition 1 with 4 rounds in the mag and 5 rounds in your second magazine. Run 50 yards or do 2X25 yard shuttle runs, do 5 push-ups or 15 jumping jacks to get your heart rate up. Immediately afterwards, at the timer beep in the standing position, draw and fire 2 rounds into the (5 point) A Zone body box of target 1. Kneel behind barrier and fire 3 rounds into the (5 point) A Zone body box of target 2. Duck down and reload, come to a kneeling position and fire 5 rounds into the (5 point) A Zone body box of target 1. Repeat 3 times. Failing to make the par time or any rounds outside the body box gives a fail for the drill.

Goals: All rounds in A box under par time.

Variations: Double the run and calisthenics once you achieve a perfect score.

3' Tall Barrier

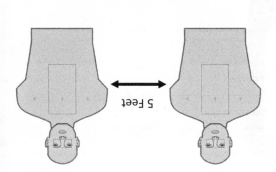

5 Feet

STREET BURNER

Date:	Location:	Weapon:	Run Distance:
Rep 1 Under Par: Y / N	Rep 2 Under Par: Y / N	Rep 3 Under Par: Y / N	# of exercises:
Total Rep 1 Time:	Total Rep 2 Time:	Total Rep 3 Time:	Notes:
All shots in A Box: Y / N	All shots in A Box: Y / N	All shots in A Box: Y / N	

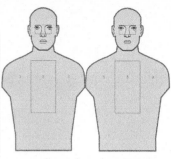

Date:	Location:	Weapon:	Run Distance:
Rep 1 Under Par: Y / N	Rep 2 Under Par: Y / N	Rep 3 Under Par: Y / N	# of exercises:
Total Rep 1 Time:	Total Rep 2 Time:	Total Rep 3 Time:	Notes:
All shots in A Box: Y / N	All shots in A Box: Y / N	All shots in A Box: Y / N	

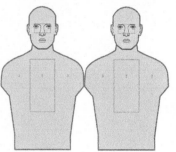

Date:	Location:	Weapon:	Run Distance:
Rep 1 Under Par: Y / N	Rep 2 Under Par: Y / N	Rep 3 Under Par: Y / N	# of exercises:
Total Rep 1 Time:	Total Rep 2 Time:	Total Rep 3 Time:	Notes:
All shots in A Box: Y / N	All shots in A Box: Y / N	All shots in A Box: Y / N	

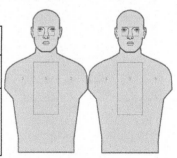

STREET BURNER

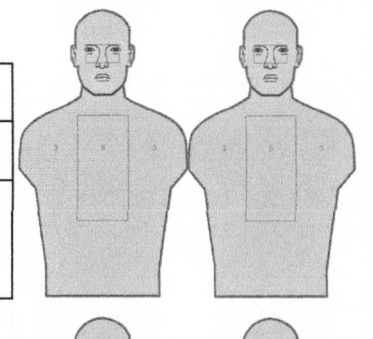

Date:	Location:	Weapon:	Run Distance:
Rep 1 Under Par: Y / N	Rep 2 Under Par: Y / N	Rep 3 Under Par: Y / N	# of exercises:
Total Rep 1 Time:	Total Rep 2 Time:	Total Rep 3 Time:	Notes:
All shots in A Box: Y / N	All shots in A Box: Y / N	All shots in A Box: Y / N	

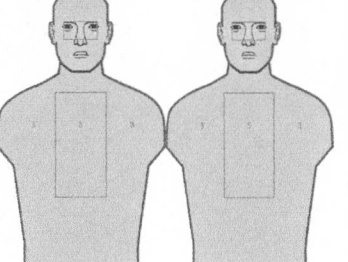

Date:	Location:	Weapon:	Run Distance:
Rep 1 Under Par: Y / N	Rep 2 Under Par: Y / N	Rep 3 Under Par: Y / N	# of exercises:
Total Rep 1 Time:	Total Rep 2 Time:	Total Rep 3 Time:	Notes:
All shots in A Box: Y / N	All shots in A Box: Y / N	All shots in A Box: Y / N	

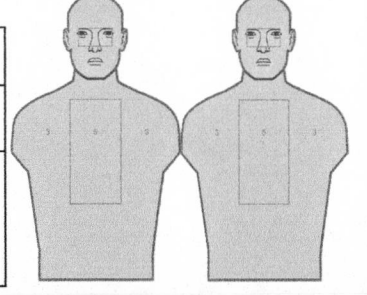

Date:	Location:	Weapon:	Run Distance:
Rep 1 Under Par: Y / N	Rep 2 Under Par: Y / N	Rep 3 Under Par: Y / N	# of exercises:
Total Rep 1 Time:	Total Rep 2 Time:	Total Rep 3 Time:	Notes:
All shots in A Box: Y / N	All shots in A Box: Y / N	All shots in A Box: Y / N	

STREET BURNER

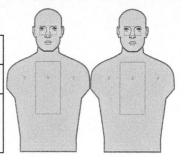

Date:	Location:	Weapon:	Run Distance:
Rep 1 Under Par: Y / N	Rep 2 Under Par: Y / N	Rep 3 Under Par: Y / N	# of exercises:
Total Rep 1 Time:	Total Rep 2 Time:	Total Rep 3 Time:	Notes:
All shots in A Box: Y / N	All shots in A Box: Y / N	All shots in A Box: Y / N	

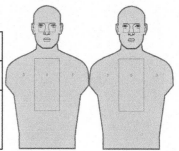

Date:	Location:	Weapon:	Run Distance:
Rep 1 Under Par: Y / N	Rep 2 Under Par: Y / N	Rep 3 Under Par: Y / N	# of exercises:
Total Rep 1 Time:	Total Rep 2 Time:	Total Rep 3 Time:	Notes:
All shots in A Box: Y / N	All shots in A Box: Y / N	All shots in A Box: Y / N	

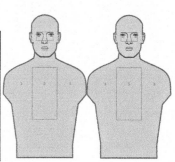

Date:	Location:	Weapon:	Run Distance:
Rep 1 Under Par: Y / N	Rep 2 Under Par: Y / N	Rep 3 Under Par: Y / N	# of exercises:
Total Rep 1 Time:	Total Rep 2 Time:	Total Rep 3 Time:	Notes:
All shots in A Box: Y / N	All shots in A Box: Y / N	All shots in A Box: Y / N	

STREET BURNER

Date:	Location:	Weapon:	Run Distance:
Rep 1 Under Par: Y / N	Rep 2 Under Par: Y / N	Rep 3 Under Par: Y / N	# of exercises:
Total Rep 1 Time:	Total Rep 2 Time:	Total Rep 3 Time:	Notes:
All shots in A Box: Y / N	All shots in A Box: Y / N	All shots in A Box: Y / N	

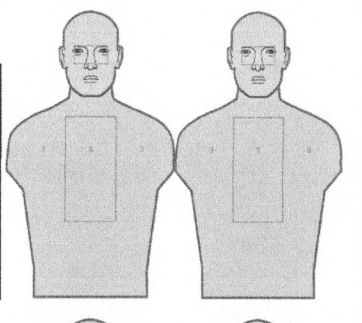

Date:	Location:	Weapon:	Run Distance:
Rep 1 Under Par: Y / N	Rep 2 Under Par: Y / N	Rep 3 Under Par: Y / N	# of exercises:
Total Rep 1 Time:	Total Rep 2 Time:	Total Rep 3 Time:	Notes:
All shots in A Box: Y / N	All shots in A Box: Y / N	All shots in A Box: Y / N	

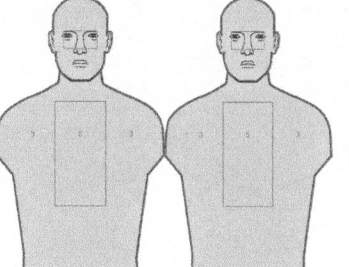

Date:	Location:	Weapon:	Run Distance:
Rep 1 Under Par: Y / N	Rep 2 Under Par: Y / N	Rep 3 Under Par: Y / N	# of exercises:
Total Rep 1 Time:	Total Rep 2 Time:	Total Rep 3 Time:	Notes:
All shots in A Box: Y / N	All shots in A Box: Y / N	All shots in A Box: Y / N	

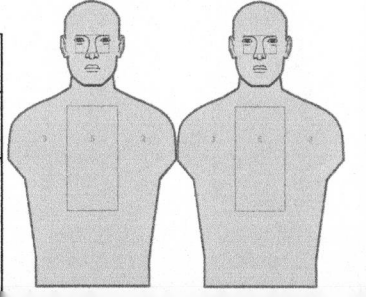

STREET BURNER

Date:	Location:	Weapon:	Run Distance:
Rep 1 Under Par: Y / N	Rep 2 Under Par: Y / N	Rep 3 Under Par: Y / N	# of exercises:
Total Rep 1 Time:	Total Rep 2 Time:	Total Rep 3 Time:	Notes:
All shots in A Box: Y / N	All shots in A Box: Y / N	All shots in A Box: Y / N	

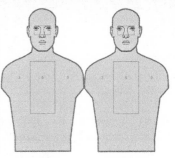

Date:	Location:	Weapon:	Run Distance:
Rep 1 Under Par: Y / N	Rep 2 Under Par: Y / N	Rep 3 Under Par: Y / N	# of exercises:
Total Rep 1 Time:	Total Rep 2 Time:	Total Rep 3 Time:	Notes:
All shots in A Box: Y / N	All shots in A Box: Y / N	All shots in A Box: Y / N	

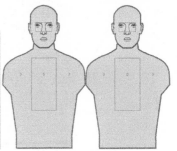

Date:	Location:	Weapon:	Run Distance:
Rep 1 Under Par: Y / N	Rep 2 Under Par: Y / N	Rep 3 Under Par: Y / N	# of exercises:
Total Rep 1 Time:	Total Rep 2 Time:	Total Rep 3 Time:	Notes:
All shots in A Box: Y / N	All shots in A Box: Y / N	All shots in A Box: Y / N	

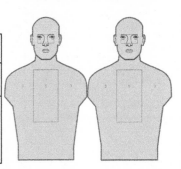

INTO THE FIGHT

Purpose: Shooting accurately while moving.

Distance: 20 Yards to 5 yards.

Target: JD-QUAL1 X 2

Par Time: 10 Seconds.

Extra Equipment Needed: Shot timer.

Rounds Fired Per Rep: 10 Rounds.   **Total Rounds Fired:** 20 Rounds.

Point Penalty: As per target score.

Repetitions: 2 Reps.

Starting Position & Condition: Standing - Surrender / Interview. Condition 1.

Description: Run 50 yards or do 2X25 yard shuttle runs, do 5 push-ups or 15 jumping jacks to get your heart rate up. Immediately afterwards, at the timer beep, draw, start walking and fire 5 rounds into the (5 point) A Zone body box of target 1, transition to target 2 and fire 5 rounds into the (5 point) A Zone body box. Repeat 2 times. Score your targets.

Goals: Failing to make the par time gives a fail for the drill. Goal is 80 points.

Variations: Double the run and calisthenics once you achieve a perfect score.

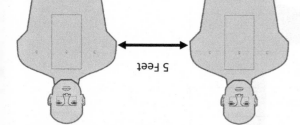

5 Feet

INTO THE FIGHT

Date:	Location:	Weapon:	Ammo:
Rep 1 Under Par: Y / N	Rep 2 Under Par: Y / N	Run Distance:	Foot Wear:
Total Rep 1 Time:	Total Rep 2 Time:	# of exercises:	Notes:
Rep 1 Score:	Rep 2 Score:	**Total Score:**	

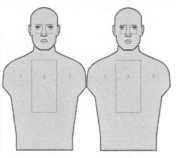

Date:	Location:	Weapon:	Ammo:
Rep 1 Under Par: Y / N	Rep 2 Under Par: Y / N	Run Distance:	Foot Wear:
Total Rep 1 Time:	Total Rep 2 Time:	# of exercises:	Notes:
Rep 1 Score:	Rep 2 Score:	**Total Score:**	

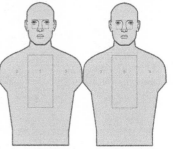

Date:	Location:	Weapon:	Ammo:
Rep 1 Under Par: Y / N	Rep 2 Under Par: Y / N	Run Distance:	Foot Wear:
Total Rep 1 Time:	Total Rep 2 Time:	# of exercises:	Notes:
Rep 1 Score:	Rep 2 Score:	**Total Score:**	

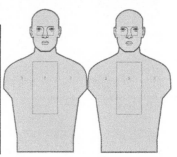

INTO THE FIGHT

Date:	Location:	Weapon:	Ammo:
Rep 1 Under Par: Y / N	Rep 2 Under Par: Y / N	Run Distance:	Foot Wear:
Total Rep 1 Time:	Total Rep 2 Time:	# of exercises:	Notes:
Rep 1 Score:	Rep 2 Score:	**Total Score:**	

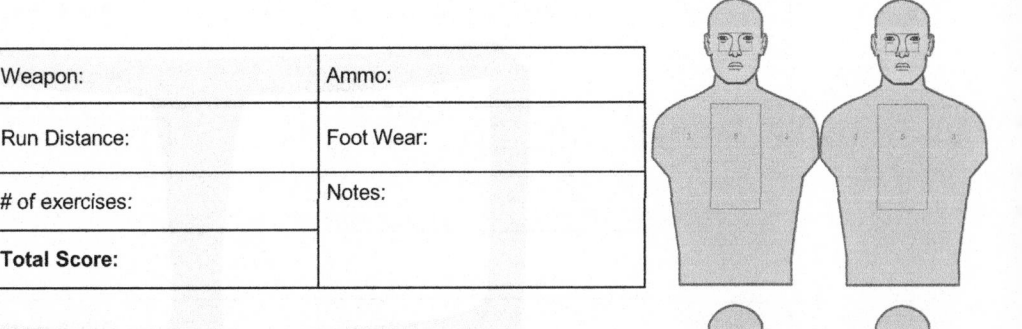

Date:	Location:	Weapon:	Ammo:
Rep 1 Under Par: Y / N	Rep 2 Under Par: Y / N	Run Distance:	Foot Wear:
Total Rep 1 Time:	Total Rep 2 Time:	# of exercises:	Notes:
Rep 1 Score:	Rep 2 Score:	**Total Score:**	

Date:	Location:	Weapon:	Ammo:
Rep 1 Under Par: Y / N	Rep 2 Under Par: Y / N	Run Distance:	Foot Wear:
Total Rep 1 Time:	Total Rep 2 Time:	# of exercises:	Notes:
Rep 1 Score:	Rep 2 Score:	**Total Score:**	

INTO THE FIGHT

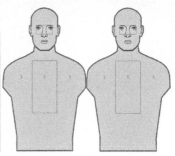

Date:	Location:	Weapon:	Ammo:
Rep 1 Under Par: Y / N	Rep 2 Under Par: Y / N	Run Distance:	Foot Wear:
Total Rep 1 Time:	Total Rep 2 Time:	# of exercises:	Notes:
Rep 1 Score:	Rep 2 Score:	**Total Score:**	

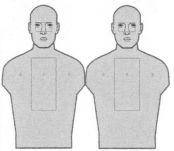

Date:	Location:	Weapon:	Ammo:
Rep 1 Under Par: Y / N	Rep 2 Under Par: Y / N	Run Distance:	Foot Wear:
Total Rep 1 Time:	Total Rep 2 Time:	# of exercises:	Notes:
Rep 1 Score:	Rep 2 Score:	**Total Score:**	

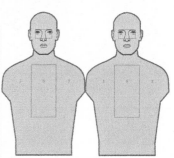

Date:	Location:	Weapon:	Ammo:
Rep 1 Under Par: Y / N	Rep 2 Under Par: Y / N	Run Distance:	Foot Wear:
Total Rep 1 Time:	Total Rep 2 Time:	# of exercises:	Notes:
Rep 1 Score:	Rep 2 Score:	**Total Score:**	

INTO THE FIGHT

Date:	Location:	Weapon:	Ammo:
Rep 1 Under Par: Y / N	Rep 2 Under Par: Y / N	Run Distance:	Foot Wear:
Total Rep 1 Time:	Total Rep 2 Time:	# of exercises:	Notes:
Rep 1 Score:	Rep 2 Score:	**Total Score:**	

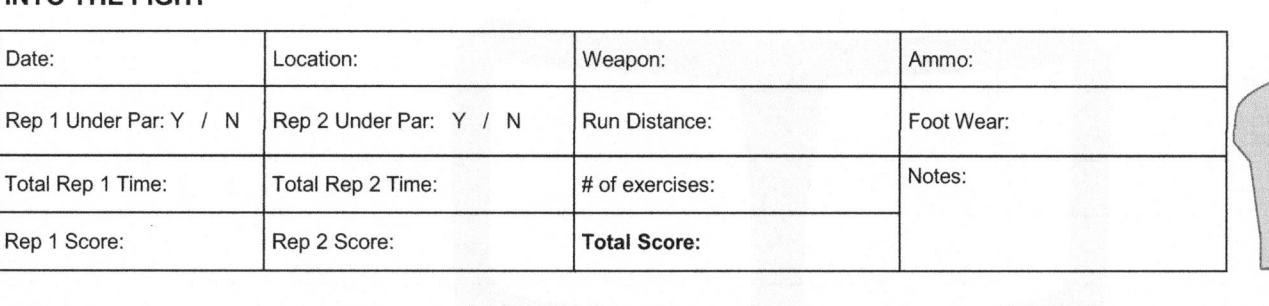

Date:	Location:	Weapon:	Ammo:
Rep 1 Under Par: Y / N	Rep 2 Under Par: Y / N	Run Distance:	Foot Wear:
Total Rep 1 Time:	Total Rep 2 Time:	# of exercises:	Notes:
Rep 1 Score:	Rep 2 Score:	**Total Score:**	

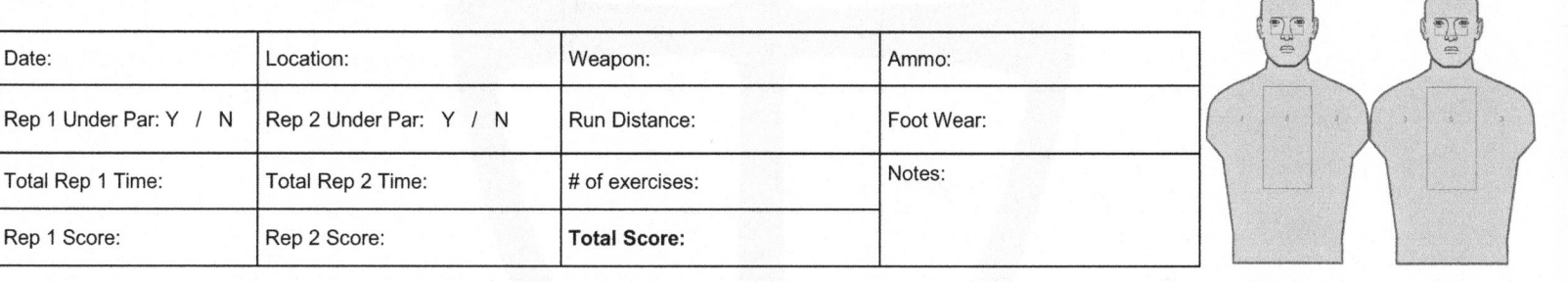

Date:	Location:	Weapon:	Ammo:
Rep 1 Under Par: Y / N	Rep 2 Under Par: Y / N	Run Distance:	Foot Wear:
Total Rep 1 Time:	Total Rep 2 Time:	# of exercises:	Notes:
Rep 1 Score:	Rep 2 Score:	**Total Score:**	

INTO THE FIGHT

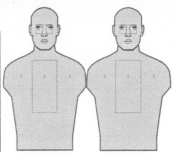

Date:	Location:	Weapon:	Ammo:
Rep 1 Under Par: Y / N	Rep 2 Under Par: Y / N	Run Distance:	Foot Wear:
Total Rep 1 Time:	Total Rep 2 Time:	# of exercises:	Notes:
Rep 1 Score:	Rep 2 Score:	**Total Score:**	

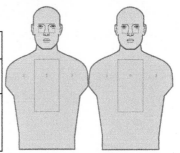

Date:	Location:	Weapon:	Ammo:
Rep 1 Under Par: Y / N	Rep 2 Under Par: Y / N	Run Distance:	Foot Wear:
Total Rep 1 Time:	Total Rep 2 Time:	# of exercises:	Notes:
Rep 1 Score:	Rep 2 Score:	**Total Score:**	

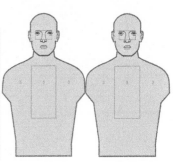

Date:	Location:	Weapon:	Ammo:
Rep 1 Under Par: Y / N	Rep 2 Under Par: Y / N	Run Distance:	Foot Wear:
Total Rep 1 Time:	Total Rep 2 Time:	# of exercises:	Notes:
Rep 1 Score:	Rep 2 Score:	**Total Score:**	

OPERATOR - Long Range Hostage

Purpose: Accuracy, stress, weapons handling.

By: Clare Ward - Marksmanship Training Center.

Distance: 3 Yards to ?

Target: Overlapping cardboard IPSC targets X 2.

Total Rounds Fired: 7 Rounds.

Starting Position & Condition: Standing - Surrender / Interview. Condition 1.

Description: Starting at 3 yards, draw and fire 1 round into the head area of a limited visibility (hostage / bad guy) target then holster and take one large step backwards. Continue this drill until you miss or hit the hostage. Record your max accurate life saving distance.

Goals: Novice: 10 yards. Expert: 20 yards. Gunfighter: 25+ yards.

Variations:

- Head A zone only.
- Fire controlled pair instead of one round.
- Add a time restraint.
- Add a side step while drawing.
- Do two push ups before drawing.

OPERATOR

Date:	Location:	Weapon:	Sights?	Notes:
From Holster? Y / N	A Zone only? Y / N	# of shots: 1 / 2	**Max Distance:**	
Date:	Location:	Weapon:	Sights?	Notes:
From Holster? Y / N	A Zone only? Y / N	# of shots: 1 / 2	**Max Distance:**	
Date:	Location:	Weapon:	Sights?	Notes:
From Holster? Y / N	A Zone only? Y / N	# of shots: 1 / 2	**Max Distance:**	
Date:	Location:	Weapon:	Sights?	Notes:
From Holster? Y / N	A Zone only? Y / N	# of shots: 1 / 2	**Max Distance:**	
Date:	Location:	Weapon:	Sights?	Notes:
From Holster? Y / N	A Zone only? Y / N	# of shots: 1 / 2	**Max Distance:**	
Date:	Location:	Weapon:	Sights?	Notes:
From Holster? Y / N	A Zone only? Y / N	# of shots: 1 / 2	**Max Distance:**	
Date:	Location:	Weapon:	Sights?	Notes:
From Holster? Y / N	A Zone only? Y / N	# of shots: 1 / 2	**Max Distance:**	
Date:	Location:	Weapon:	Sights?	Notes:
From Holster? Y / N	A Zone only? Y / N	# of shots: 1 / 2	**Max Distance:**	
Date:	Location:	Weapon:	Sights?	Notes:
From Holster? Y / N	A Zone only? Y / N	# of shots: 1 / 2	**Max Distance:**	

OPERATOR

Date:	Location:	Weapon:	Sights?	Notes:
From Holster? Y / N	A Zone only? Y / N	# of shots: 1 / 2	Max Distance:	

Date:	Location:	Weapon:	Sights?	Notes:
From Holster? Y / N	A Zone only? Y / N	# of shots: 1 / 2	Max Distance:	

Date:	Location:	Weapon:	Sights?	Notes:
From Holster? Y / N	A Zone only? Y / N	# of shots: 1 / 2	Max Distance:	

Date:	Location:	Weapon:	Sights?	Notes:
From Holster? Y / N	A Zone only? Y / N	# of shots: 1 / 2	Max Distance:	

Date:	Location:	Weapon:	Sights?	Notes:
From Holster? Y / N	A Zone only? Y / N	# of shots: 1 / 2	Max Distance:	

Date:	Location:	Weapon:	Sights?	Notes:
From Holster? Y / N	A Zone only? Y / N	# of shots: 1 / 2	Max Distance:	

Date:	Location:	Weapon:	Sights?	Notes:
From Holster? Y / N	A Zone only? Y / N	# of shots: 1 / 2	Max Distance:	

Date:	Location:	Weapon:	Sights?	Notes:
From Holster? Y / N	A Zone only? Y / N	# of shots: 1 / 2	Max Distance:	

Date:	Location:	Weapon:	Sights?	Notes:
From Holster? Y / N	A Zone only? Y / N	# of shots: 1 / 2	Max Distance:	

OPERATOR

Date:	Location:	Weapon:	Sights?	Notes:
From Holster? Y / N	A Zone only? Y / N	# of shots: 1 / 2	**Max Distance:**	
Date:	Location:	Weapon:	Sights?	Notes:
From Holster? Y / N	A Zone only? Y / N	# of shots: 1 / 2	**Max Distance:**	
Date:	Location:	Weapon:	Sights?	Notes:
From Holster? Y / N	A Zone only? Y / N	# of shots: 1 / 2	**Max Distance:**	
Date:	Location:	Weapon:	Sights?	Notes:
From Holster? Y / N	A Zone only? Y / N	# of shots: 1 / 2	**Max Distance:**	
Date:	Location:	Weapon:	Sights?	Notes:
From Holster? Y / N	A Zone only? Y / N	# of shots: 1 / 2	**Max Distance:**	
Date:	Location:	Weapon:	Sights?	Notes:
From Holster? Y / N	A Zone only? Y / N	# of shots: 1 / 2	**Max Distance:**	
Date:	Location:	Weapon:	Sights?	Notes:
From Holster? Y / N	A Zone only? Y / N	# of shots: 1 / 2	**Max Distance:**	
Date:	Location:	Weapon:	Sights?	Notes:
From Holster? Y / N	A Zone only? Y / N	# of shots: 1 / 2	**Max Distance:**	
Date:	Location:	Weapon:	Sights?	Notes:
From Holster? Y / N	A Zone only? Y / N	# of shots: 1 / 2	**Max Distance:**	

Date:	Location:	A Zone only? Y / N	From Holster? Y / N	Notes:
Sights?	Weapon:	# of shots: 1 / 2	**Max Distance:**	
Date:	Location:	A Zone only? Y / N	From Holster? Y / N	Notes:
Sights?	Weapon:	# of shots: 1 / 2	**Max Distance:**	
Date:	Location:	A Zone only? Y / N	From Holster? Y / N	Notes:
Sights?	Weapon:	# of shots: 1 / 2	**Max Distance:**	
Date:	Location:	A Zone only? Y / N	From Holster? Y / N	Notes:
Sights?	Weapon:	# of shots: 1 / 2	**Max Distance:**	
Date:	Location:	A Zone only? Y / N	From Holster? Y / N	Notes:
Sights?	Weapon:	# of shots: 1 / 2	**Max Distance:**	
Date:	Location:	A Zone only? Y / N	From Holster? Y / N	Notes:
Sights?	Weapon:	# of shots: 1 / 2	**Max Distance:**	
Date:	Location:	A Zone only? Y / N	From Holster? Y / N	Notes:
Sights?	Weapon:	# of shots: 1 / 2	**Max Distance:**	
Date:	Location:	A Zone only? Y / N	From Holster? Y / N	Notes:
Sights?	Weapon:	# of shots: 1 / 2	**Max Distance:**	
Date:	Location:	A Zone only? Y / N	From Holster? Y / N	Notes:
Sights?	Weapon:	# of shots: 1 / 2	**Max Distance:**	

OPERATOR

Date:	Location:	Weapon:	Sights?	Notes:
From Holster? Y / N	A Zone only? Y / N	# of shots: 1 / 2	**Max Distance:**	
Date:	Location:	Weapon:	Sights?	Notes:
From Holster? Y / N	A Zone only? Y / N	# of shots: 1 / 2	**Max Distance:**	
Date:	Location:	Weapon:	Sights?	Notes:
From Holster? Y / N	A Zone only? Y / N	# of shots: 1 / 2	**Max Distance:**	
Date:	Location:	Weapon:	Sights?	Notes:
From Holster? Y / N	A Zone only? Y / N	# of shots: 1 / 2	**Max Distance:**	
Date:	Location:	Weapon:	Sights?	Notes:
From Holster? Y / N	A Zone only? Y / N	# of shots: 1 / 2	**Max Distance:**	
Date:	Location:	Weapon:	Sights?	Notes:
From Holster? Y / N	A Zone only? Y / N	# of shots: 1 / 2	**Max Distance:**	
Date:	Location:	Weapon:	Sights?	Notes:
From Holster? Y / N	A Zone only? Y / N	# of shots: 1 / 2	**Max Distance:**	
Date:	Location:	Weapon:	Sights?	Notes:
From Holster? Y / N	A Zone only? Y / N	# of shots: 1 / 2	**Max Distance:**	
Date:	Location:	Weapon:	Sights?	Notes:
From Holster? Y / N	A Zone only? Y / N	# of shots: 1 / 2	**Max Distance:**	

GUNFIGHTER PISTOL STANDARD 1

- **Ammo:** 1 magazine of 4 rounds, 1 mag of 10 rounds, 1 mag of 11 round.   25 Rounds total.

- **Target:** JD-QUAL1

- **Scoring:** As per target score. Subtract 5 points for any shot over time. Passing score is 110 out of 125 points

- **Draw:** Each stage requires a Condition 1 draw from concealment. Holster after each stage.

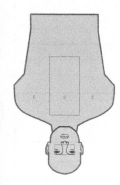

Stage	Distance	#Rnds	Time	Position/Description
1	3 Yards	1	2 Sec	1 round to A zone HEAD box.
2	3 Yards	2	2 Sec	2 rounds to A zone BODY box.
3	7 Yards	1 + 1	4.5 Sec	1 round to A zone body box. Reload. 1 round to A zone body box.
4	7 Yards	3	3.5 Sec	2 rounds to A zone BODY box. 1 round to A Zone HEAD box.
5	7 Yards	6	5 Sec	6 rounds to A zone BODY box. (Reload with 11 round - not timed)
6	25 Yards	10	15 Sec	10 rounds to A zone BODY box.
7	25 Yards	1	5 Sec	1 round to A zone HEAD box.

GUNFIGHTER PISTOL STANDARD 1

Date:	Location:	Holster: Concealed / Duty / Open	
Weapon:	Sights:	Ammo:	Day / Night
Stage 1: 1 Round - 2 Sec.	Draw Time:	Stage Time:	Score:
Stage 2: 2 Rounds - 2 Sec.	Draw Time:	Stage Time:	Score:
Stage 3: 1+1 Rounds - 4.5 Sec.	Draw Time:	Stage Time:	Score:
Stage 4: 3 Rounds - 3.5 Sec	Draw Time:	Stage Time:	Score:
Stage 5: 6 Rounds - 5 Sec.	Draw Time:	Stage Time:	Score:
Stage 6: 10 Rounds - 15 Sec.	Draw Time:	Stage Time:	Score:
Stage 7: 1 Round - 5 Sec.	Draw Time:	Stage Time:	Score:
Notes:			**Total Score:**

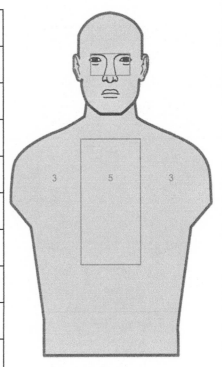

GUNFIGHTER PISTOL STANDARD 1

Date:	Location:	Holster: Concealed / Duty / Open	
Weapon:	Sights:	Ammo:	Day / Night
Stage 1: 1 Round - 2 Sec.	Draw Time:	Stage Time:	Score:
Stage 2: 2 Rounds - 2 Sec.	Draw Time:	Stage Time:	Score:
Stage 3: 1+1 Rounds - 4.5 Sec.	Draw Time:	Stage Time:	Score:
Stage 4: 3 Rounds - 3.5 Sec	Draw Time:	Stage Time:	Score:
Stage 5: 6 Rounds - 5 Sec.	Draw Time:	Stage Time:	Score:
Stage 6: 10 Rounds - 15 Sec.	Draw Time:	Stage Time:	Score:
Stage 7: 1 Round - 5 Sec.	Draw Time:	Stage Time:	Score:
Notes:			**Total Score:**

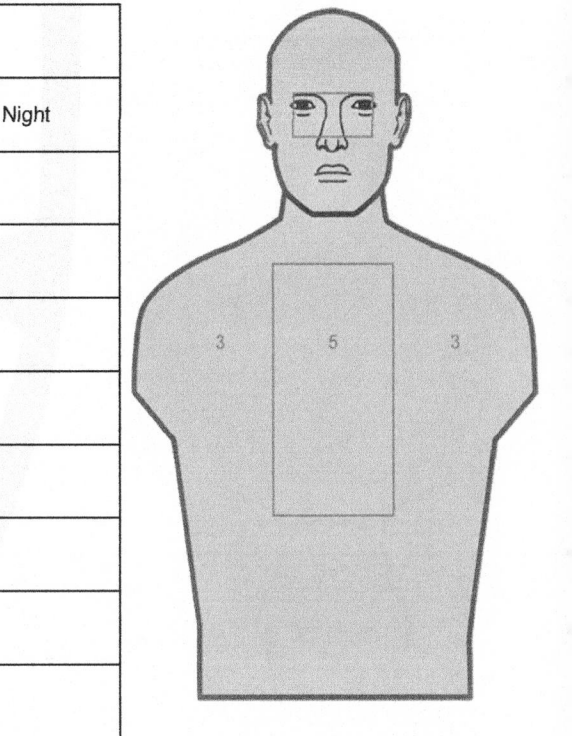

GUNFIGHTER PISTOL STANDARD 1

Date:	Location:	Holster: Concealed / Duty / Open	
Weapon:	Sights:	Ammo:	Day / Night
Stage 1: 1 Round - 2 Sec.	Draw Time:	Stage Time:	Score:
Stage 2: 2 Rounds - 2 Sec.	Draw Time:	Stage Time:	Score:
Stage 3: 1+1 Rounds - 4.5 Sec.	Draw Time:	Stage Time:	Score:
Stage 4: 3 Rounds - 3.5 Sec	Draw Time:	Stage Time:	Score:
Stage 5: 6 Rounds - 5 Sec.	Draw Time:	Stage Time:	Score:
Stage 6: 10 Rounds - 15 Sec.	Draw Time:	Stage Time:	Score:
Stage 7: 1 Round - 5 Sec.	Draw Time:	Stage Time:	Score:
Notes:			**Total Score:**

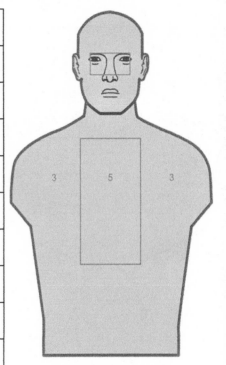

GUNFIGHTER PISTOL STANDARD 1

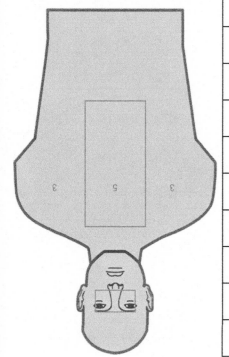

Date:	Location:	Holster: Concealed / Duty / Open	
Weapon:	Sights:	Ammo:	Day / Night
Stage 1: 1 Round - 2 Sec.	Draw Time:	Stage Time:	Score:
Stage 2: 2 Rounds - 2 Sec.	Draw Time:	Stage Time:	Score:
Stage 3: 1+1 Rounds - 4.5 Sec.	Draw Time:	Stage Time:	Score:
Stage 4: 3 Rounds - 3.5 Sec.	Draw Time:	Stage Time:	Score:
Stage 5: 6 Rounds - 5 Sec.	Draw Time:	Stage Time:	Score:
Stage 6: 10 Rounds - 15 Sec.	Draw Time:	Stage Time:	Score:
Stage 7: 1 Round - 5 Sec.	Draw Time:	Stage Time:	Score:
Notes:			Total Score:

GUNFIGHTER PISTOL STANDARD 1

		Holster: Concealed / Duty / Open	
Date:	Location:		
Weapon:	Sights:	Ammo:	Day / Night
Stage 1: 1 Round - 2 Sec.	Draw Time:	Stage Time:	Score:
Stage 2: 2 Rounds - 2 Sec.	Draw Time:	Stage Time:	Score:
Stage 3: 1+1 Rounds - 4.5 Sec.	Draw Time:	Stage Time:	Score:
Stage 4: 3 Rounds - 3.5 Sec	Draw Time:	Stage Time:	Score:
Stage 5: 6 Rounds - 5 Sec.	Draw Time:	Stage Time:	Score:
Stage 6: 10 Rounds - 15 Sec.	Draw Time:	Stage Time:	Score:
Stage 7: 1 Round - 5 Sec.	Draw Time:	Stage Time:	Score:
Notes:			**Total Score:**

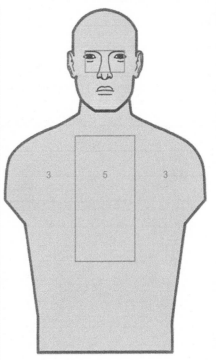

GUNFIGHTER PISTOL STANDARD 2

- **Ammo:** 3 magazines of 15 rounds + 15 loose rounds. 60 Rounds total.

- **Target:** JD-QUAL1. All shots in A Zone (5 point) body box, unless noted.

- **Scoring:** As per target score. Subtract 5 points for any shot over time. Passing score is 270 out of 300 points.

- **Draw:** Each stage requires a Condition 1 draw from concealment, unless noted. Reholster after each stage.

Stage	Distance	#Rnds	Time	Position/Description
1	50 Yards	5	25 Sec	Standing to prone, kneeling or standing (shooters choice).
2	35 Yards	5	18 Sec	Standing to kneeling.
3	25 Yards	5 + 5	20 Sec	5 rounds standing. Speed reload. 5 rounds kneeling.
	Clear, make ready with mag of 15 rounds. Secure the ejected mag of 10 rounds.			
4	25 Yards	15	35 Sec	5 rounds standing. 5 rounds kneeling. 5 rounds standing. (reload previous 10 round mag.)
5	10 Yards	5	10 Sec	Standing to kneeling to HEAD ONLY.
6	10 Yards	5	7 Sec	Standing LOW READY. Emergency reload.
7	7 Yards	2	1.3 Sec	Standing LOW READY.
8	5 Yards	3 + 2	8 Sec	Standing HIGH READY. 3 rounds. Reload. 2 rounds.
9	5 yards	8	10 Sec	Standing LOW READY to HEAD ONLY.

GUNFIGHTER PISTOL STANDARD 2

Date:	Location:	Holster: Concealed / Duty / Open	
Weapon:	Sights:	Ammo:	Day / Night
Stage 1: 5 Rounds - 25 Sec.	Draw Time:	Stage Time:	Score:
Stage 2: 5 Rounds - 18 Sec.	Draw Time:	Stage Time:	Score:
Stage 3: 5+5 Rounds - 20 Sec.	Draw Time:	Stage Time:	Score:
Stage 4: 15 Rounds - 35 Sec.	Draw Time:	Stage Time:	Score:
Stage 5: 5 Rounds - 10 Sec.	Draw Time:	Stage Time:	Score:
Stage 6: 5 Rounds - 7 Sec.	Draw Time:	Stage Time:	Score:
Stage 7: 2 Rounds - 1.3 Sec.	Draw Time:	Stage Time:	Score:
Stage 8: 3+2 Rounds - 8 Sec	Draw Time:	Stage Time:	Score:
Stage 9: 8 Seconds - 10 Sec.	Draw Time:	Stage Time:	Score:
Notes:			**Total Score:**

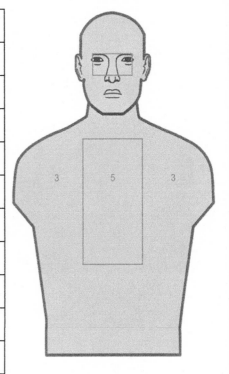

GUNFIGHTER PISTOL STANDARD 2

Date:	Location:	Holster: Concealed / Duty / Open	
Weapon:	Sights:	Ammo:	Day / Night
Stage 1: 5 Rounds - 25 Sec.	Draw Time:	Stage Time:	Score:
Stage 2: 5 Rounds - 18 Sec.	Draw Time:	Stage Time:	Score:
Stage 3: 5+5 Rounds - 20 Sec.	Draw Time:	Stage Time:	Score:
Stage 4: 15 Rounds - 35 Sec.	Draw Time:	Stage Time:	Score:
Stage 5: 5 Rounds - 10 Sec.	Draw Time:	Stage Time:	Score:
Stage 6: 5 Rounds - 7 Sec.	Draw Time:	Stage Time:	Score:
Stage 7: 2 Rounds - 1.3 Sec.	Draw Time:	Stage Time:	Score:
Stage 8: 3+2 Rounds - 8 Sec	Draw Time:	Stage Time:	Score:
Stage 9: 8 Seconds - 10 Sec.	Draw Time:	Stage Time:	Score:
Notes:			**Total Score:**

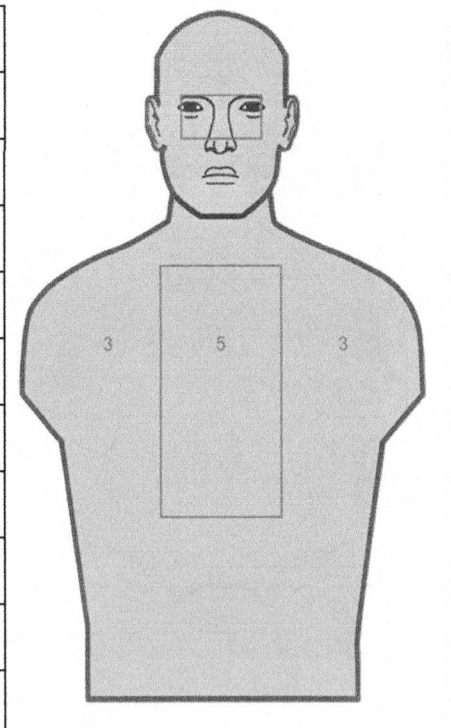

GUNFIGHTER PISTOL STANDARD 2

		Holster: Concealed / Duty / Open	
Date:	Location:		
Weapon:	Sights:	Ammo:	Day / Night
Stage 1: 5 Rounds - 25 Sec.	Draw Time:	Stage Time:	Score:
Stage 2: 5 Rounds - 18 Sec.	Draw Time:	Stage Time:	Score:
Stage 3: 5+5 Rounds - 20 Sec.	Draw Time:	Stage Time:	Score:
Stage 4: 15 Rounds - 35 Sec.	Draw Time:	Stage Time:	Score:
Stage 5: 5 Rounds - 10 Sec.	Draw Time:	Stage Time:	Score:
Stage 6: 5 Rounds - 7 Sec.	Draw Time:	Stage Time:	Score:
Stage 7: 2 Rounds - 1.3 Sec.	Draw Time:	Stage Time:	Score:
Stage 8: 3+2 Rounds - 8 Sec	Draw Time:	Stage Time:	Score:
Stage 9: 8 Seconds - 10 Sec.	Draw Time:	Stage Time:	Score:
Notes:			**Total Score:**

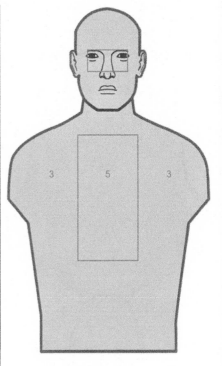

GUNFIGHTER PISTOL STANDARD 2

Date:	Location:	Holster: Concealed / Duty / Open	
Weapon:	Sights:	Ammo:	Day / Night
Stage 1: 5 Rounds - 25 Sec.	Draw Time:	Stage Time:	Score:
Stage 2: 5 Rounds - 18 Sec.	Draw Time:	Stage Time:	Score:
Stage 3: 5+5 Rounds - 20 Sec.	Draw Time:	Stage Time:	Score:
Stage 4: 15 Rounds - 35 Sec.	Draw Time:	Stage Time:	Score:
Stage 5: 5 Rounds - 10 Sec.	Draw Time:	Stage Time:	Score:
Stage 6: 5 Rounds - 7 Sec.	Draw Time:	Stage Time:	Score:
Stage 7: 2 Rounds - 1.3 Sec.	Draw Time:	Stage Time:	Score:
Stage 8: 3+2 Rounds - 8 Sec	Draw Time:	Stage Time:	Score:
Stage 9: 8 Seconds - 10 Sec.	Draw Time:	Stage Time:	Score:
Notes:			**Total Score:**

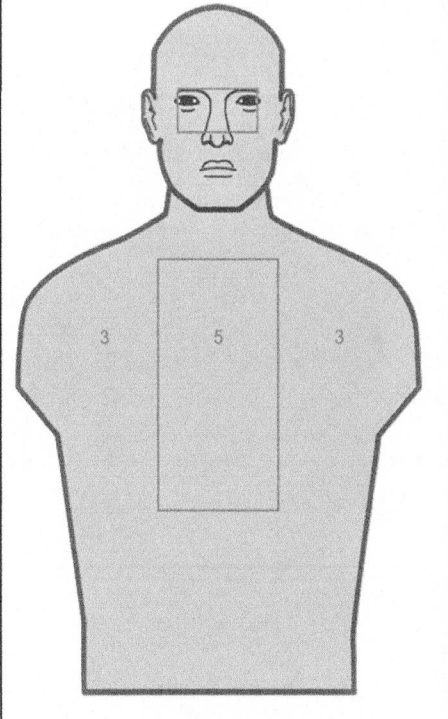

GUNFIGHTER PISTOL STANDARD 2

		Holster: Concealed / Duty / Open	
Date:	Location:		
Weapon:	Sights:	Ammo:	Day / Night
Stage 1: 5 Rounds - 25 Sec.	Draw Time:	Stage Time:	Score:
Stage 2: 5 Rounds - 18 Sec.	Draw Time:	Stage Time:	Score:
Stage 3: 5+5 Rounds - 20 Sec.	Draw Time:	Stage Time:	Score:
Stage 4: 15 Rounds - 35 Sec.	Draw Time:	Stage Time:	Score:
Stage 5: 5 Rounds - 10 Sec.	Draw Time:	Stage Time:	Score:
Stage 6: 5 Rounds - 7 Sec.	Draw Time:	Stage Time:	Score:
Stage 7: 2 Rounds - 1.3 Sec.	Draw Time:	Stage Time:	Score:
Stage 8: 3+2 Rounds - 8 Sec	Draw Time:	Stage Time:	Score:
Stage 9: 8 Seconds - 10 Sec.	Draw Time:	Stage Time:	Score:
Notes:			**Total Score:**

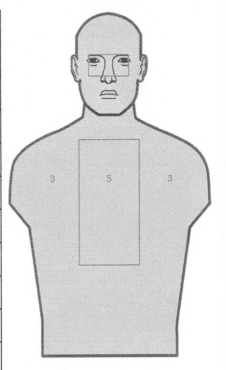

NAME OF CUSTOM DRILL:

Purpose:

By:

Distance: Yards

Target:

Par Time: Seconds

Extra Equipment Needed:

Rounds per Repetition: Rounds

Total Rounds Fired: Rounds

Point Penalty:

Repetitions:

Starting Position & Condition: Start in the

Description:

Goals: Novice: **Expert:** Gunfighter:

Variations:

Custom Drill Name:

Date:	Location:	Weapon:	Sights:	Ammo
				Notes:
Date:	Location:	Weapon:	Sights:	Ammo
				Notes:
Date:	Location:	Weapon:	Sights:	Ammo
				Notes:
Date:	Location:	Weapon:	Sights:	Ammo
				Notes:
Date:	Location:	Weapon:	Sights:	Ammo
				Notes:

Custom Drill Name:

Date:	Location:	Weapon:	Sights:	Ammo
Notes:				
Date:	Location:	Weapon:	Sights:	Ammo
Notes:				
Date:	Location:	Weapon:	Sights:	Ammo
Notes:				
Date:	Location:	Weapon:	Sights:	Ammo
Notes:				
Date:	Location:	Weapon:	Sights:	Ammo
Notes:				

Custom Drill Name:

Date:	Location:	Weapon:	Sights:	Ammo
				Notes:
Date:	Location:	Weapon:	Sights:	Ammo
				Notes:
Date:	Location:	Weapon:	Sights:	Ammo
				Notes:
Date:	Location:	Weapon:	Sights:	Ammo
				Notes:
Date:	Location:	Weapon:	Sights:	Ammo
				Notes:

NOTES:

NOTES:

Training Classes Taken

Date:	Institute:	Class Name:	Weapon:

Notes about subjects covered:

_____

_____

_____

Notes about equipment used:

_____

_____

_____

Instructors Name:	Contact Info:
Instructors Name:	Contact Info:
Students Name:	Contact Info:
Students Name:	Contact Info:
Students Name:	Contact Info:
Students Name:	Contact Info:
Students Name:	Contact Info:

Training Classes Taken

Date:	Institute:	Class Name:	Weapon:

Notes about subjects covered:

_____

_____

_____

Notes about equipment used:

_____

_____

_____

_____

Instructors Name:	Contact Info:
Instructors Name:	Contact Info:
Students Name:	Contact Info:
Students Name:	Contact Info:
Students Name:	Contact Info:
Students Name:	Contact Info:
Students Name:	Contact Info:

Training Classes Taken

Date:	Institute:	Class Name:	Weapon:

Notes about subjects covered:

Notes about equipment used:

Instructors Name: Contact Info:

Instructors Name: Contact Info:

Students Name: Contact Info:

Students Name: Contact Info:

Students Name: Contact Info:

Students Name: Contact Info:

Students Name: Contact Info:

Training Classes Taken

Date:	Institute:	Class Name:	Weapon:

Notes about subjects covered:

_____

_____

_____

Notes about equipment used:

_____

_____

_____

Instructors Name: _____ Contact Info: _____

Instructors Name: _____ Contact Info: _____

Students Name: _____ Contact Info: _____

Students Name: _____ Contact Info: _____

Students Name: _____ Contact Info: _____

Students Name: _____ Contact Info: _____

Students Name: _____ Contact Info: _____

Training Classes Taken

Date:	Institute:	Class Name:	Weapon:

Notes about subjects covered:

_____

_____

Notes about equipment used:

_____

_____

_____

_____

Instructors Name:	Contact Info:
Instructors Name:	Contact Info:
Students Name:	Contact Info:
Students Name:	Contact Info:
Students Name:	Contact Info:
Students Name:	Contact Info:
Students Name:	Contact Info: